YOUR PARISH PRIEST, A MAN OF MYSTERY

To, Alice –

Please pray for more priests.

Your Parish Priest, A Man of Mystery

Msgr. Dermot R. Brennan

Msgr. Dermot R. Brennan

ST PAULS

Library of Congress Cataloging-in-Publication Data

Brennan, Dermot R.
  Your parish priest : a man of mystery / Dermot R. Brennan.
       p. cm.
   ISBN 978-0-8189-1293-1
   1. Priests—United States. 2. Catholic Church—United States—Clergy. 3.
Priesthood—Catholic Church. 4. Pastoral theology—Catholic Church.   I. Title.
   BX1912.B75 2009
   262'.142—dc22
                              2008038771

Produced and designed in the United States of America by the
Fathers and Brothers of the Society of St. Paul,
2187 Victory Boulevard, Staten Island, New York 10314-6603
as part of their communications apostolate.

ISBN 10: 0-8189-1293-6
ISBN 13: 978-0-8189-1293-1

Printing Information:

Current Printing - first digit   1   2   3   4   5   6   7   8   9   10

Year of Current Printing - first year shown

2009   2010   2011   2012   2013   2014   2015   2016   2017   2018

Acknowledgments

I wish to thank the following for reading the text and providing many valuable insights and suggestions:

Msgr. John Doherty, Msgr. Robert Panke, Fr. Luke Sweeney, Sister Marie Pappas, CR, John and Gabrielle Toman, Tricia Jarrell and Lorraine and Gary Suraci.

In addition, I express my sincerest thanks to all the priests who have provided direction, inspiration, leadership, wisdom and friendship throughout my life and thereby contributed greatly to my growth as a priest. May there be many more like them in the years ahead.

Table of Contents

Introduction

It was late on a Sunday evening in May. I had celebrated three of our nine weekend Masses, heard Confessions for an hour, celebrated two weddings and performed seven baptisms. I was at my desk checking my calendar to see what the next day held for me when the phone rang. I picked it up and said, "St. Patrick's, Fr. Brennan." A very irate woman responded, "You have some nerve changing the Mass schedule without telling us! I was late for Mass this morning and it was your fault!" I was tired and not ready for such an aggressive call but, keeping my temper in check, I explained. "I'm sorry that you missed Mass, but we have been announcing those changes for the past four weeks both in the weekly Bulletin and at every weekend Mass." Not giving me an inch and obviously not wishing to accept my explanation, she went on to state, "I have been away for the last four weeks." Doing all I could to conceal my exasperation, I repeated, "Well, I'm sorry that you missed Mass but I feel we did everything we could to get the word out. I'd be happy to give you the adjusted schedule now." No less belligerently, she countered with, "You don't have to do that, I can pick up a copy of the Bulletin during the week." I thought she was done but she went on, "While I have you on the phone, I want to ask you a question. Besides saying Mass every day and going to the hospital once in awhile, what do you guys do all week anyhow?"

Tired and a bit annoyed, I nonetheless decided to answer the question. Because I was at my desk and checking my calendar, I said, "Well, let me tell you what I have scheduled for tomorrow. First, I'll be up at 6 o'clock to celebrate the 6:55 AM Mass. After the Mass I will anoint someone who is going to the hospital for surgery on Tuesday and then I will go to the chapel to make my Holy Hour before the Blessed Sacrament. After I have breakfast and glance through the newspaper, I will go over to the school to teach two Religion classes. When I return to the rectory, I'll pick up any phone messages and return those calls. I'll probably skip lunch because I have a meeting with some of the priests of the area followed by a one hour staff meeting. Monday is my day to go to the local hospital so I'll spend an hour or so there, then return to go through my mail and put aside until tomorrow any letters that require a response. Then it's time for dinner, after which I have a Parish Council meeting that will last a couple of hours. After the meeting I'll stop in at the chapel again, and then lock up the church in time to get back to my room and perhaps catch the last couple of innings of a ball game on TV or write one or two of those letters. And that all presumes that there will be no drop-in visits from parishioners during the day. And that's what I'll be doing on Monday. Would you like to hear about Tuesday?" There was silence at the other end for a moment and then the woman said, "I'm sorry, Father, if I embarrassed you by your having to tell me all that." I could not resist saying, "I really think you embarrassed yourself, not me, but have a pleasant evening and I hope to see you at Mass next weekend." (I confessed my snide remark the next time I went to Confession.)

That incident has stayed with me for over a dozen years and is really what is behind my writing this book. I have often thought that there are probably a lot of Catholics out there who have no idea of exactly what we priests do between Sunday evening and Saturday morning. Indeed, there are probably a lot of people who wonder why we became priests in the first place and what we see in and get out of this life. So the title, *Your Parish Priest, A Man of Mystery,* actually addresses our life on two levels.

The first is the level of sacred mystery, that level which is most obvious to most Catholics. It is the level that involves the priest in the essential works for which he is ordained, namely, to be Christ to the people whom he is called to serve. Essentially, we are talking about celebrating Mass and the seven Sacraments and joining in the Liturgy of the Hours prayed by the universal Church each day. According to theological expression, he is called to act *in persona Christi,* "in the person of Christ," and in doing so, he shares in a very special way in the mysteries of Christ's life and the mystery of the life of His Church which we often call "the Mystical Body of Christ." It is there where he reaches his people on the highest level possible given to humans, living out the presence of God within *all* of us that originates with our Baptism and the resulting sharing in the life of God's grace which we will define in detail in the first part of the book. The very significant impact all of this has on the priest's daily and personal life will be examined in detail.

The other level of mystery is a response to the question sometimes asked openly, more often internally, "What does my parish priest do between Sunday evening and Saturday morning?" or as my late night caller put it, "What do you guys do all week anyway?" It is hoped that my responses to these questions will enable the reader to come away with a greater appreciation of how busy and very fulfilling the life of a parish priest can be in today's Catholic Church. It is further hoped that, in this day of an increasing shortage of candidates for the priesthood, the contents of this work might inspire some younger unmarried men to consider whether God might be calling them to enter the Catholic priesthood in order to serve God's people on these two levels of "mystery."

Please bear in mind that the thoughts and observations that follow are those of one now retired priest who is the product of an urban background and a large archdiocesan seminary, much of which I will share with you as we go along. However, given the admitted differences between life in the Archdiocese of New York and another diocese of suburban or almost totally rural life, I feel confident that the essentials are always there. As a matter of fact, in the New York archdiocese there is not a single kind of ministry that a priest cannot experience, from rural to suburban life, from the poverty and mixed ethnicity of the inner city to upscale apartment or expensive suburban living, from hospital ministry to being part of a high school faculty, from dealing with the homeless and the well-to-do or being part of the archdiocesan administration. A Catholic priest is ordained to serve all God's People and, in a real and basic way, those whom he is called to serve are seeking a closer relationship with God just as the priest is. In short, the results of the mysteries they celebrate together make an impact on the daily lives we all live. So a priest is a priest wherever and to whomever he is called upon to serve.

However, since the mid-sixties, and primarily as a result of some major writings produced by the Second Vatican Council (1962-65), the parish priest is also called upon to lead and support the laity as they grow in their awareness that, by the very fact of their baptism, they, too, share in the priesthood of Jesus, though in a manner different from that of the ordained priest. It has become increasingly evident in light of both the teachings of the Council and the growing shortage of priests, that in our time the laity are called to play increasingly more important roles in the life of their Church. No longer are they simply to "pray, pay and obey"; we know now that they are called to a more active and cooperative involvement with their pastor in the life of the parish and even to assume a role of leadership in the planning and carrying out of specific activities that serve to enliven and energize the modern parish family.

My hope is that you the reader will finish this book with a deeper understanding of and even a greater love for those who have answered the call to shepherd the Lord's flock. At the same time, my prayer is that you will grow personally in your appreciation of the role that you, as a layperson, must fulfill if the Catholic Church is not only to continue its outstanding work but flourish even more.

About the Author or Who Am I?

To put all of the observations that will follow into proper perspective, an overview of my background might prove helpful since the person we are and the ideas and principles by which we live are largely the product of the family, education and geographic area in which we grow up. It will be in synopsis form since the most pivotal stories will be detailed in several of the following chapters.

My beginnings were on the island of Manhattan in New York City where I was born on May 22, 1930, the second of the four sons of Michael and Mary A. (Molly) Brennan. My parents were unusual Irish immigrants for that time since they were both college graduates, my father from Galway College where he would go on to teach Mathematics, and my mother from the Royal Academy of Music in Dublin where she majored in piano and voice. They came to the U.S. in 1926 "to see America" but following the birth of their first son in 1928 and then the Wall Street "Crash" in 1929, neither would see Ireland again until my father returned in 1954, and then my mother in 1961 when the three of us made the journey "home."

After brief stays in Astoria and midtown, they settled on the upper West Side of Manhattan, bringing them within the boundaries and lifelong influence of Corpus Christi Parish. The pastor, Fr. George B. Ford, was somewhat of a rebel and certainly a forward looking man in many aspects of his pastoring. Upon taking over the parish in 1935, he undertook the construction in one building of a brand new colonial-style church, school, auditorium and convent and brought in the Dominican Sisters of Sinsinawa, Wisconsin to staff the school. They advocated what Fr. Ford wanted: a form of education which focused on discovering the student's individual gifts, fostering thinking, creative writing, public speaking and the arts and sciences, rather than on memorization and rote recitation of names, dates and places. My present love for reading, writing and music were given a strong foundation in that atmosphere and the older I get, the more I appreciate and am grateful for the eight years I spent at Corpus Christi School.

Fr. Ford also put great emphasis on the parish liturgy. Under his leadership, the Mass celebrated each weekend, contained several components that clearly anticipated the changes that came in 1967. Small wonder that when the liturgical changes came the parishioners of Corpus Christi parish were well prepared. Moreover, Fr. Ford was very much in the forefront in the areas of social justice and inter-faith activities. Following his lead, the upper grades of the school often did projects or took part in debates on the current social issues such as housing, segregation and racism, thus making us quite aware of a much larger life outside our parish. Growing up in our extraordinary parish with its wonderful priests and in a strong Catholic home where my father was a daily communicant and we prayed the Family Rosary every evening during October and May, it was not thought unusual that one of the four Brennan boys would enter the priesthood.

So following graduation from Corpus Christi School, I entered Cathedral College, the preparatory seminary. From there I moved on to the major seminary, St. Joseph's, in Yonkers, New York from which I was ordained in 1956, one of forty-one new priests that year. My first assignment was to St. Peter's in Liberty, New York, approximately ninety-five miles north of the City. Essentially rural, it was in the heart of the Catskill Mountains. It was my first experience of life outside the City and I loved it. As my first parish, it was also where I really began to learn how to be a priest!

Fifteen months into that period, the pastor had a massive stroke and I was left in charge of the parish for the next seven months during which time we were building a brand new parochial school. In time there were problems with the construction which I reported to the proper church authorities and soon a pastor was assigned, his last name being the same as mine! With the confusion this caused and the fact that I was there longer than he was, I could sense a change in the offing. Sure enough, in August, I was assigned back to Manhattan to teach at Bishop Dubois High School, a small school of five hundred boys on the upper West Side. Arriving just three weeks before the opening of school, I met the principal and asked, "What do you want me to teach?" He responded, "Latin I and II." I said, "Fine, but you need to know that I took Latin for six years in the prep seminary and failed it three times." His reply? "Then you'll understand the kids' problems!"

My first year as a teacher was a disaster. I wanted to be in parish work, preferably back in St. Peter's, but the principal, Msgr. Michael Buckley, a wonderful, intense little Irishman, urged me to stay on for at least one more year and also suggested that I get a Masters Degree. I thought I could get out of that by suggesting that it be in Music Education (I had a fairly strong background in music) but, much to my surprise, the Chancellor, Msgr. Terence Cooke (later Cardinal Cooke), gave his approval. I began studies at Teachers College, Columbia University in 1959 and, while still working towards the degree, was transferred in 1960 to Cardinal Hayes High School to become Head of the Music Department. I spent ten happy years there teaching Latin II, Religion, Advanced Band, Concert Band, Music Appreciation and Chorus. But during that time the Second Vatican Council took place (1962-65); there were real changes coming about and I wanted to be back in a parish "where the action was."

So I went to the newly established Priest Personnel Board and asked to be reassigned to a parish. During my twelve years teaching I had helped out on weekends at Sts. Peter and Paul parish in the South Bronx where I learned that I do not have a gift for languages and Spanish was now becoming a requirement if one was to successfully minister in a New York inner-city parish. So when the Board asked, "Where would you like to work?" I responded, "Anywhere but inner-city," giving the reason. That resulted in my being assigned to Immaculate Heart of Mary Parish in Scarsdale, N.Y., a middle- to upper-class parish where I was privileged to work with three great pastors, all of whom included me in their decision-making and taught me a great deal. It was a period of real personal growth and taught me how important a role a pastor can play in the training of younger priests.

After ten years there (during which I also served as Chairman of the Archdiocesan Music Commission, was a member of the Liturgy Commission and taught the Church Music course at the Seminary), I received a call from Fr. Charles McDonough, the Cardinal's Secretary, on December 22, 1979. "The Cardinal wants to see you tomorrow," he said. I protested that the next day we had four hours of pre-Christmas Confessions scheduled. He repeated, "The Cardinal wants to see you tomorrow." Then I took the plunge and asked, "What does he want to see me about?" I received an answer I will never forget: "Dermot, I just drive the truck, I don't deliver the packages!"

The "package" Cardinal Cooke delivered to me was my first pastorate at Our Lady of Victory Parish in Mount Vernon, a small middle class city in southern Westchester County. The parish was ethnically mixed: predominantly Italian, some Irish and German and a steadily growing Portuguese community. It was at Our Lady of Victory that I had a spiritual experience that would change my life, but more about that later.

After five years in Mt. Vernon, I received a call from the Personnel Board asking me to consider becoming the pastor of a large parish in northern Westchester. The circumstances surrounding the fulfillment of that request will also be dealt with later on. Suffice it to note here that, once again, God cleared the way for me to do what *He* wanted me to do instead of what *I* wanted to do. Twenty years later, after leading the parish through a growth from 3,400 registered families to 4,750, I was "burned out" and put in for retirement at age 75. At this writing I am living at the John Cardinal O'Connor Clergy Residence in the Riverdale section of the Bronx, with thirty-three other priests, almost all older than I. I am kept busy helping out in a nearby parish on weekends, celebrating Mass three days a week at a residence for retired Marist Brothers, reading, writing, praying, accepting invitations to preach when they come, visiting long-time friends, and trying to be present to my nine nephews and nieces and their families since I'm the only survivor of the four Brennan boys. I also have time for continuing with my hobby of performing Magic and doing an occasional workshop on a previously authored book, *Homilies Kids Can See* (published by Our Sunday Visitor Press). It contains forty homilies that use visuals that are easily obtainable or can be made of basic materials following the detailed instructions provided. It deals with the reality that today's children have a very short attention span and visuals are needed to hold their attention and deliver the message. A number of the homilies are also appropriate for adults given that they, too, live in a world of visuals.

So that's who I am and where I have come from, not everyman's story but containing enough variety, along with some peaks and valleys, to validate sharing some thoughts on *Your Parish Priest, a Man of Mystery.*

With that background, let's move on to the twofold "mystery" of being a parish priest as I, together with my brothers in the priesthood, have lived it, with some insights into how it might change in the years ahead.

YOUR PARISH PRIEST, A MAN OF MYSTERY

PART ONE

The Priest as Minister of God's Mysteries

Chapter 1

The Mystery of God's Call to Priesthood

In today's post-Vatican II theological climate, the term "vocation," which in the past referred almost exclusively to those called to the priesthood or religious life, has been extended to include every baptized person, and rightly so. After all, in the baptismal ceremony, immediately after the priest has poured water on the head of the person, he anoints them with a special oil called chrism and states, "I anoint you priest, prophet and king." It is then that we all begin to share in the mysteries of the life of Jesus. By being anointed as priest we are all called to share in the office of priesthood, not in the sense of being ordained specifically to that life but because we are called to share in the sacrificial and sacramental life of the Church through which the mysteries of Christ are celebrated and lived out in our daily lives.

We are also called to be prophets, a term too often misunderstood as referring exclusively to the ability to foretell the future. Rather, the term, "prophet" comes from the Greek which means "to speak for another," and in the case of the Old Testament prophets and John the Baptist in the New Testament, they were, of course, speaking for God. It is in that sense that all of the baptized are called to be prophets, that is, we are empowered to lead others to God through our words and/or deeds, as long as they are in tune with the teachings of Jesus and His Church. With that understanding, we can see the wisdom in the inspiring words of St. Francis of Assisi when he urged his followers to "Preach the gospel whenever possible; if necessary, use words!"

The third vocation to which we are called by our baptismal anointing is that of king. By this two things are understood. First, we are called to be children of the Kingdom, living the life to which Jesus has called us in such a way as to reveal our commitment to Him. Secondly, we are empowered by God's grace to choose His will over ours when we would rather do ours. In a sense, then, we are king over our own destiny, not that we can control what happens to us in our lives but that we are empowered to respond to it as God would have us respond by allowing His grace to direct our choices.

When viewed from this baptismal perspective, then, *every* baptized Christian has been called, has been given a vocation, to live as God has called us to live, and He provides the grace we need to do that. This applies to everyone, single, married, professed religious and ordained priest. However, the call to the vocation of *priesthood* is a unique one that directs a man to be, as we have said, what the theologians call, "another Christ," and that will be the fundamental thrust of the observations we will share. So, how does this call come and how does a man know it is for him? What exactly are these "mysteries" that a priest is called to celebrate and how does his role in their celebration render him unique while still being very human?

Clearly, these questions will be addressed but first, let's begin by making three things very clear.

First, no man decides on his own to become a priest. As the Letter of St. Paul to the Hebrews tells us, "No one takes this honor on himself." So it is God who does the choosing and the man who chooses to respond, but the initiative is always with God. After all, it is *His* priesthood in which a man is called to share, not some human institution, profession or career that we decide to pursue.

Second, no man deserves to be called to the priesthood no matter how holy he might appear to be. During my fifty years of ministry, it has been my delight to encounter many men whom I would judge to be far holier than I, beginning with my father and my brothers and extending that judgment to many other laymen with whom it has been my privilege to share my ministry. Trust me, this is not false modesty; this is the truth. There are many laymen and professed religious (i.e., brothers and sisters) whom I have met who have impressed me enormously with the manner in which they bring to their daily lives the teachings of Jesus, sometimes to a depth that leads to my embarrassment. So holiness is that virtue which enables every person to strive each day to do the will of God as best they can in whatever situation they are in at the time, but that striving is always in response to the energizing grace of God.

Third, as I go through the rest of this volume, I will cite a number of examples and stories to clarify or illustrate a point being made. Because the priestly life I know best is my own, many of those illustrations will be from my own experience. In addition, the names of the other people in the stories will be changed but all the details will follow what happened.

CHAPTER 2

Basic
Qualifications

I t has been customary to say that there are three signs of a possible vocation to the priesthood: (1) a good moral and spiritual life, (2) a degree of intelligence coupled with an ongoing desire to learn, and (3) sufficiently good health to withstand the rigors of the daily life of a priest.

The good moral life indicates that a man is already waging the difficult daily war to resist the temptations of the world and to grow spiritually in his life, fundamentally through daily prayer and meditation as well as a commitment to the moral teachings of Jesus and His Church. There should be at least the beginnings of a desire to encounter Christ in his life and to discern how the Lord wants him to serve Him. The fact that a man becomes a priest in no way lessens his humanity so, just as any layperson or vowed religious will make an ongoing effort to deepen his/her life in Christ, and can do so only with the constant in-pouring of God's grace, so the priest will need the special graces of his calling to achieve that goal.

Intellectually, his school records should indicate that he possesses sufficient intelligence to study and grasp the many academic subjects required to successfully complete seminary studies. These would include Philosophy, Dogmatic and Moral Theology, Sacred Scripture, Church Law, Church History, Liturgy, Homiletics (the art of delivering a good presentation based on the Scripture Readings of the day or liturgical season), and any other subject deemed necessary according to local needs, e.g., learning a second language to deal with those in his diocese who come from non-English speaking countries.

Physically, it should be clear that, especially in light of today's diminishing number of priests being ordained in the United States, a candidate for priesthood should be in good physical health with no ongoing illnesses or debilitating conditions. Indeed, many dioceses have launched health programs specifically for their priests in order to provide the means and incentives for them to maintain their health and thereby meet the rigors resulting from an active ministry.

I personally would add a fourth requirement. I speak of the spirit of generosity. By this is meant an abiding spirit of service and self-sacrifice on behalf of the people he is called to serve. If Jesus tells us that the sign of a true friend is the willingness to lay down his life for his friend, then surely the priest ought to be willing to put aside his own temporal desires to serve those people whom he has been ordained to serve. My mentor often reminded me and other priests whom he guided, that we are to be visible and available and to empower the people to fulfill their baptismal call to serve. Does that mean that the priest should have no time for himself? Of course not. To do that is to invite early burnout and a shorter term of ministry than he could give, to say nothing of doing physical and/or emotional damage to himself.

However, it does mean that his life is to be spent in loving, *sacrificial* service to the particular people whom he has been called to serve. It means attempting to do whatever one can do to be "another Christ" to those who are in need of his priestly service, whatever form that might take at a given time and situation. The priesthood is not a job, nor a career or a profession and sometimes it will call for a 24/7 regimen in response to the needs, often unpredictable, of his people. Nonetheless, he must take care of himself so as to be able to fulfill all the demands of his call.

CHAPTER 3

Whom Does God Call?

Were you to ask this question of ten priests you would probably get ten different answers. The reason? Each one of us is a unique individual coming from individual backgrounds and living in individual circumstances. There is no "typical" priest. If there were, then you could spot the "right person" to the degree that they fit the "typical" personality, character and circumstances. This was quite clearly indicated when our parish launched a low key but somewhat effective program which reached out to some young men to encourage them to consider whether the Lord might be calling them to priesthood. First the three priests in the parish got together to draw up a list of the high school boys we thought were likely candidates, drawing from their family background (faithful Mass attendance, a good marriage) and their involvement in parish activities. These might include serving at the altar, singing in the choir, participating in the youth program, being active in their Catholic high school, volunteering in our Religious Ed program, etc. We also sought input from the members of our parish staff, especially those whose roles cause them to interact with these young men.

After sending each of them an invitation to dinner and offering them several dates, they came in small groups, usually two to four boys. (We also gave them the option of respectfully declining the invitation which several did.) The dinner was a simple one, usually spaghetti and meatballs and some popular dessert, and it was accompanied by conversation, usually about their school work, sports, family happenings, etc. Toward the end of the meal, I and the other two priests shared the stories of our vocations, starting with our family life at their age and then telling how we heard and answered the call. As it turned out, each story was significantly different.

As you already know, I was what we in New York call a "lifer," that is, a fellow who went to the prep seminary and college, then the major seminary and, following ordination, out to a parish. By contrast, the youngest of the three went to public grammar school and high school in suburbia, and then entered the seminary. After a year, he was sent to Rome to study but was quite unhappy there and returned to the States, leaving the seminary. A year later, he re-entered and after completing a couple more years, still wasn't sure that God was calling him, so he left again. As he puts it, "I got cold feet." However, he went to work with a priest friend in inner-city Manhattan, a pastor known for his involvement with the poor, including local public housing. After a year there, the young man re-entered the seminary and was ordained, coming to our parish as his first assignment. That whole process produced a man who, in my estimation, is one of the finest young priests that I have ever encountered, with a natural instinct for ministry. As I write, he is serving in one of the largest parishes in the archdiocese and doing wonderful work.

The third man is a convert from the Lutheran faith. His

academic education was entirely secular and he worked for a time as an economist for the federal government in Washington, D.C. Following his conversion to Catholicism in his late forties, he felt called to the priesthood. He applied to a seminary that specializes in what were then called, "delayed" vocations. This is a term that really no longer applies since many newly ordained priests in America now come to the seminary after spending some time in the professional world. He was accepted by the bishop of a Midwest diocese and sent to Rome where he completed his studies. After ordination, he served that diocese for five years, but as his mother, who lived in Maryland, was advancing in years, he wished to serve in an area closer to her. He applied to New York, was accepted and assigned to our parish. Now in his mid-fifties, he feels a special call to teach young people their faith. So, besides doing his daily service in the parish, he also teaches at least one class of Religion each day in a local Catholic high school.

Those three totally different stories were found quite interesting by the young men who heard them and, if nothing else, they indicated clearly that there is no one path to the priesthood. God will call those whom He wishes to serve. It is their role to listen and respond. Given the young age of those boys who were present at the dinner, I do not know whether they will give further consideration to whether God is calling them to priesthood but we priests at least had the satisfaction of knowing that we made a specific effort to introduce them to the idea. I hope that my successors will continue the invitation and that others may make similar efforts. If we do not invite them, they may not even think about a priestly vocation, let alone respond to one.

In the past two decades we have seen an increase in the age at which men enter the seminary. Prior to Vatican II it was very common that the average newly ordained priest would be in his mid-twenties. Today it is more likely that he be in his thirties or forties. The reasons are several. Some have large student loans to pay off before they can enter; others try some profession or other occupation before they realize that they will find fulfillment only in the priesthood. A few want to make sure that their parents are cared for, especially if they are ill, and some just need time to come to that final decision. Whatever the reason, once they determine that the Lord is calling them to priestly service, their journey begins with time in the seminary for study and final discernment.

It should now be clear, then, that there is no "typical" candidate for priesthood. Each man called has a unique personality and background with a unique combination of special gifts that the Lord wishes him to use in His service and that of His Church. To the degree that each man responds with a generous heart, the image of Christ will gradually take form in his heart, mind and will and he will be formed by God's grace into the man God wishes him to be.

Someone has suggested humorously that if the twelve men called to be Apostles had submitted their resumes for evaluation to the Jordan Management Consultants, the results might have been as follows: "Peter is too emotional and given to fits of temper; and his brother Andrew has no sense of leadership. James and John place personal interest above company loyalty and Thomas' questioning attitude would undermine company morale. Matthew, the tax collector, is currently blacklisted by the Greater Jerusalem Better Business Bureau and both James (Alphaeus' son) and Thaddeus, aka Nathaniel, reveal radical tendencies and registered high scores as manic depressives. However, one of the candidates shows great ability and resourcefulness, is a great net-worker with a keen business mind, is adept in financial matters and has strong contacts with people in high positions. We recommend Judas Iscariot as your Controller and Chief Operating Officer and wish you well in your new venture." So clearly there is no "typical" candidate for priesthood. The Lord chooses whom He will and molds and shapes them into fitting instruments for His work.

CHAPTER 4

How Does the
Call Come?

As we have seen, the call to priesthood comes in a variety of ways, just as it did to the Apostles. Responding to Jesus' invitation, "Follow me!" some of them were recruited from their jobs as fishermen, two of them brought their brothers, and another was a tax collector who worked for the despised Roman government. The previous occupations of the other Apostles we simply do not know. What is clear is that they were called and, at first, they revealed none of the classic indicators we outlined above. But Jesus wanted them, He called them and they answered. Over a three year period (their seminary training!), He shaped them to be able to endure the apparent failure of His Passion, rejoice and have their faith confirmed in His Resurrection, and then, filled with the Holy Spirit on Pentecost, go out to proclaim the Good News that is Jesus to all the nations. They gave their lives to Him and achieved the goal that the Lord had set for them before the world was created. But how does that happen in our time?

Certainly the call comes through prayer. Since it is God who does the calling, the vocation to the priesthood will come when the young man is in communication with Him. God will speak to him in his heart and gradually draw the man to Him and, if the one He is calling is listening, then He will take the lead and show him the way. This call can be further strengthened through the invitation of a parent, sibling, relative, or parishioner and/or through the inviting word and example of a priest who is living his priesthood to the fullest.

I have already told you the story of two of my associates in my former parish, indicating how very different their paths to priesthood were. Let me share with you in more detail my own story and then that of another much younger man.

As far back as I can remember, whenever anyone asked me when I first thought about becoming a priest, I always answered, "I've wanted to be a priest since second grade," not really ever knowing why. How was that vocation seed planted? Here's the story. While in second grade, I became very sick with double pneumonia and pleurisy. One of the priests of the parish, Fr. Joseph P. Moore (who would later become the chaplain at West Point Military Academy, then a pastor and who is now deceased), visited me at home. While there, he must have asked me if I had ever thought of becoming a priest. I say, "must have asked me" because I don't actually recall his doing so. However, he must have done so because, after I responded in whatever way I did, he must have turned to my younger brother, Norm, and asked him the same question. His response? "Don't look at me, Fr. Moore!" an expression which became part of the Brennan family folklore, usually uttered when a volunteer for a family chore was being sought. Now fast forward to November 3, 1982 when I was lined up in procession with many other priests entering St. Joseph's Church in Bronxville, New York to celebrate the Mass of Christian Burial for Msgr. Moore, the pastor. It was then that it all came together. He was the one who had planted the seed that led me so often to say, "Since second grade" whenever I was asked about when I first thought about becoming a priest.

What a great lesson that was and I have thought of it many times since then whenever I have asked some young man, "Have you ever thought about becoming a priest?" That's a question that needs to be asked over and over in these times of a severe priest shortage. Too many times have I heard or read about a priest who would have responded to the call earlier in life if someone had only invited him.

The other story is of a young man who grew up in a solid Catholic family of seven children; five girls and two boys. His father was a surgeon, his mother an actively devout parishioner. There was always a sense of service of others encouraged both in word and example by the parents. Today, three of the daughters are nurses, each of them active in a specialized field. The younger of the two boys attended the local public grammar school and high school, and then went to the Catholic University of America in the nation's capitol. Upon graduation, he stayed in Washington, D.C. to work but had no clear idea what he wanted to do, not an unusual occurrence in today's world. He did know he wanted to serve others in some way. His parents were going on a pilgrimage to Medjugorje, something they had done twice previously. It is alleged that the Blessed Mother appears regularly in this village in Croatia to deliver her Son's messages to the world. I have been there and was greatly moved by the villagers, the multitude of pilgrims and the devotion revealed by all present at the liturgies. Since the young man had no specific plans for the summer, they encouraged him to go along, and somewhat halfheartedly, he did. This young college grad came home, rather pensive and reflective. Not long afterwards, and much to their delight, he let his parents know that he had decided to enter the seminary. He chose the Washington, D.C. Archdiocese where he had gone to school and worked and is doing outstanding priestly work there today.

The conclusion? If God wants a man to be a priest, He will do everything He can to break through into the young man's world and extend the invitation. It can come in his heart as God speaks to him in prayer; it can come through the influence of a priest or priests whom he admires; it can come through the spoken encouragement of a friend or relative. ("Have you ever thought about being a priest? I think you would make a good one.") If the young man is listening in prayer and to the encouragement and invitation of his parish priests, family and friends, then he will know that the call is real and he may be sure that God will bless him with all the graces that he will need to respond with a generous heart.

The next step will be to enter the seminary to test that call, and that involves no commitment; it simply makes real his determination to see if the priesthood is really what God wants of him. His time there will either solidify his vision or help him determine that God has other plans for him. Either way, it will be a very profitable experience.

CHAPTER 5

Other
Influences

I n addition to the example and encouragement of the parish priests upon the youth in regard to pursuing a vocation to the priesthood or religious life, the children of my time (pre-Vatican II) had the great influence of the religious sisters and/or brothers in their lives, especially if they went to Catholic parochial schools. Often it was those outstanding people, who themselves were living the vows of poverty, chastity and obedience, who frequently were the principal influences on those youth whom they thought showed the signs of a vocation to the priesthood or religious life. Sadly, along with the number of priests now serving the Catholic Church in America, the number of religious brothers and sisters has diminished greatly so that their influence is no longer as strong as it once was. Who is to take their place, then, in encouraging today's young men to think about the priesthood as a calling? The answer is the laity, and especially the parents and siblings of possible candidates. In light of the negative publicity that a very few priests (less than 2%) have brought on the priesthood in today's America, together with a secular and consumer society that measures success according to how much money one can earn and how many possessions one can gather, too many parents and others who could possibly influence a young man toward the priesthood fail to do so. They don't see priesthood as a worthwhile option.

I recall two such instances, one which took place following the graduation of a very fine Catholic young man from college. I remarked to his father, "You know, your son would make a wonderful priest." His answer? "Father, I just spent almost a hundred thousand dollars on his education and now you want him to become a *priest*?" Stopped only for a moment, I responded, "Well, thanks for the insult!" A bit flustered, he went on, "I'm sorry, Father. I didn't mean to insult you," to which I said, "Perhaps you didn't intend it but your implication is that a priest isn't worth that much of an investment." I feel confident in saying that, in today's society, this gentleman was not alone in his evaluation. Those who spell "success" as $ucce$$ are not in a minority and, whether they realize it or not, they thereby see the priesthood as a poor investment, at least for their own sons.

The other instance of a negative attitude toward priesthood on the part of parents was simply stated in the response I received to the same remark I made about another possible candidate, "Your son would make a fine priest." Their reply? "Father, we have other plans for him." And I simply asked, "But what about *God's* plans for him?" That is really what parenting is supposed to be about, namely, to prepare one's children to determine what plan God has in mind for them and then assist and encourage them to complete it because, apart from that call, they will find no real lasting happiness.

One last thought before moving on. It is the role of each Catholic to do whatever can be done to encourage and pray for young men to answer the call to serve the Church in the priesthood. If more lay people who see a young man who seems to be a worthwhile candidate would simply tell him that and say, "I'll pray for you each day to know whether God is calling you," we could quite possibly see a steady increase in the number of those who respond to Christ's call to be His representative to His people through priestly ministry. Indeed, Canon 233, paragraph 1 of the Code of Canon Law officially states that families, educators and priests are called to encourage young people to seriously consider whether God is calling them into His service. It is clearly everyone's responsibility.

I recall a priest friend of mine saying to his congregation when they were commenting on the influx of priests from other cultures and some of the resulting difficulties, "If you want American priests then give us American priests!" A blunt statement? Yes. A very provocative and meaningful challenge? Absolutely—and one that needs to be seriously considered by all Catholic laity. I encourage you, the reader, to undertake such an apostolate and to apply it to young women, too, encouraging them to consider whether God might be calling them to the consecrated life as a sister or nun.

Having reviewed the steps by which a man can determine whether he has been called to priesthood and presuming that he has responded and been ordained to the ministry, let us now examine his life as a priest, a *man of mystery*, beginning with that first level of mystery, his life in Christ.

CHAPTER 6

Sharing in the Mysteries of Christ

The words "Liturgy" and "Priesthood" can almost be taken as synonymous. It is in the celebration of the liturgy that the priest touches the essential function of his ministry. All else flows from these celebrations. However, too often, the word "liturgy" is used only in reference to the celebration of the Mass, which fails to take into account the many other aspects of liturgy. In order to understand the depth of the priest's calling—and that of all those who share with him in the celebration of the various forms of liturgy—we need to understand precisely what liturgy is.

As was so well presented by Clifford Howell, S.J. in his now-out-of print masterpiece, *Of Sacraments and Sacrifice,* the word "liturgy" comes from a Greek word which means "a public work by an individual for the common good in which all people share." In its original meaning, liturgy applied essentially to acts of philanthropy. For example, to finance and build a gymnasium, a theater, a school, a library or some other public edifice would be a liturgical act. It was a public act (the erection of the building) by an individual (the donor) for the common good (the surrounding community) in which all the people could share. We see the same principle in action today when someone makes a large donation to a hospital, a concert hall, a university. According to the root meaning of the word, they are performing a liturgical act.

Then Jesus came and gave a whole new meaning to the word. We might say that He caused it to be spelled with a capital "L." For when we examine His entire life, not just His Passion, Death, and Resurrection as renewed in each Mass, but all His life from Conception to Ascension, then we are confronted with the ultimate liturgical act. Consider the following.

Were we to ask ourselves what were the most significant events and actions in the life of Jesus, that is, His liturgical actions, we would probably begin with His Passion, Death, and Resurrection, those momentous actions by which He redeemed the entire world. This is why He came; this was the ultimate goal for which the Father sent Him. But what else did He do? Among other things, He stated that He had come to give us life to the fullest. Further, He forgave sins, He healed the sick, He sent the Holy Spirit to strengthen and guide His followers, He sent men out to preach His Word, and He even sanctified the union of man and woman in marriage by raising that union to be a sign of the union in Himself of His two natures, human and divine, a union motivated by His infinite love for all.

What we actually have listed here are the Mass and the seven Sacraments. They are, in summary, the principal acts in the life of Jesus continued in our time through the ministry of the Church. Let us briefly look at each and consider the role played by the priest in each as he acts in the person of Christ.

As an aside, we understand that an ordained deacon can also baptize and officiate at marriages, but this is an office created not by Christ but by the Church under the guidance of the Holy Spirit, and one only recently revived in the life of the Church. Some Vocation Directors have shared that from time to time a young man will express the desire that he might want to be a priest but would also like to be married so he is thinking about pursuing the permanent diaconate. It is important that he understand an essential difference.

The permanent deacon's life most often is joined to or follows upon a worldly career as well as marriage and raising a family. On the other hand, the ordained priest gives his life totally to Christ and His Church in a lifelong service of celebrating the Mass and Sacraments, preaching the Word of God and leading his people to the life of service to which they were called at their Baptism.

To return to our consideration of the life of grace, it is important for our purpose to understand precisely what grace is since its infusion into our souls, in various forms, is the essential reason for the existence of each of the sacraments. For many, especially those trained in the era prior to the Second Vatican Council, to be "in the state of grace" means to have no serious sin on one's soul, which is correct. However, that tells us what grace is *not*; it is not sin. But what is it? I would define it as a supernatural gift of God by which He infuses into our soul a real share in His very own divine life. Therefore, grace is God living in and through us so that He may use us, *all* of us who are baptized, as His instruments in this world to proclaim by our lives His presence and His saving work in the world. So grace is not just the absence of sin from our souls; rather, it is the presence of God in our souls. Just as Jesus came to make the Father visible to us, so Jesus comes to live in us so we can make Him visible to our world through our grace-energized thoughts, words and actions. Sometimes when I am celebrating a Baptism, the infant is still and quiet until the water is poured on its head; then it squalls. To lighten the moment, especially for the parents who may be embarrassed, I will say to those present, "That's just the devil going out of the child!" But, in saying so, I'm also reinforcing the point of God's life being poured into that child at that very moment. Jesus referred to this very special presence in John's Gospel (chapter 15) when He described Himself as the Vine and us as the branches, a figure He did not choose casually. From that image we deduce that the very same life principle that flows through the vine flows *unchanged* into the branches which cannot have life unless they are grafted onto the vine. Indeed, those branches which do not bear fruit will be "cut off and thrown into the fire" precisely because they are not alive with the life of the Vine. By this real inner presence of God, we become something sacred and holy because we are now truly an instrument of God, animated by this remarkable gift by which we share in His divine life.

In our Church, for instance, incense is sometimes used at celebrations to show special honor to a person or thing as well as to symbolize our prayers rising to the Father in heaven. So, at a Mass of Christian Burial, the celebrant incenses five things because they are holy. He incenses the altar on which the sacrifice takes place, the bread and wine which are to become Jesus' Body and Blood, the crucifix which is the great sign of God's love for the whole world, the Paschal Candle which is the symbol of the Risen Jesus, and the body of the deceased person. Why the last? Because, since that person's Baptism, his or her body has been a temple or dwelling place of the Holy Trinity. Therefore, our bodies are the instruments through which Jesus reveals Himself to those whose lives we touch.

The letters of St. Paul are replete with references to this

inner life of grace, perhaps none more specific than that in the Letter to the Galatians (2:20) in which he declares, "The life I live is no longer mine, it is Christ who lives in me. I continue to live my natural life but with an abiding belief in Christ who lives in me." No wonder we often call a Baptism a "Christening" since, through it, we are made newly alive with Christ's life so that, for the rest of our days, we can reveal His presence within us. Therefore, we can truly say that in Baptism we are "born again," given a whole new level of life, just as Jesus said we must be. "Unless you are born again of water and the Holy Spirit, you cannot have life in you." (John 3:5) Indeed, the word "supernatural," which we use to describe grace, means "above the natural." In other words, when we receive that share in God's divine life, we are thereby enabled to live a life on a whole new level, above the merely natural. It is the presence of God's grace within us that makes that supernatural life possible.

So essential is this new life in God that the Lord also confers a special outpouring of grace in the Sacrament of Confirmation. What is actually "confirmed" or strengthened is the person's Baptism. The bestowal of the many gifts of the Spirit are intended to energize the Christian so he can consistently—and sometimes even bravely—reveal God's inner presence by choosing God's will over his own and conquering the temptations to which he is exposed. Further on we will consider the role of the priest in the celebration of each of the Sacraments but for now let's continue to look at them in summary fashion.

In spite of our having been born anew and then strengthened in God's life of grace, the effects of Original Sin are still within us resulting in our making choices contrary to God's will. However, the reality of our sinfulness is countered with the Sacrament of Penance in the Rite of Reconciliation. The rebirth of Baptism removes Original Sin, but the effects of that primal disobedience by our first parents are still present so that our intellect is darkened and our will is weakened. The result is that we are all sinners in need of God's forgiveness which He willingly grants to those who admit their sinfulness and call on His mercy, thereby restoring or increasing His grace in our souls.

We are weak, frail human beings who are often in need of physical or emotional healing, the gift of inner peace through our acceptance of our suffering. In cases where our suffering results in depression or even despair, the Lord is ready to heal us at least inwardly and does so through the sign of His healing, the Sacrament of the Anointing of the Sick.

The Most Blessed of all these sacraments is, of course, the Holy Eucharist which is both sacrament and sacrifice, making it possible for us to re-present the Passion, Death, and Resurrection of Jesus under the appearance of the consecrated bread and wine in each celebration of the Mass. Through it we can not only offer Jesus to the Father in atonement for our sins but we can then receive Him whom we have offered as our Food, in order to sustain and strengthen us in our daily efforts to do His will. In short, we can become Him whom we offer and consume. In light of this extraordinary gift, I have often said to people who have left the Church or at least stopped going to Mass, "You obviously have what you consider good reasons for your conduct, but I have to ask you one very important question: 'How can you walk away from the Eucharist if you really believe that it is Jesus who is offered and received? Don't you miss what no other religion can offer you?'"

The incarnation of our God and His offering of His life for our salvation is the greatest sign we have of His love for us. Through it He united to His divine nature a human nature, taken from the womb of the Blessed Virgin Mary. This union was motivated by His eternal and unconditional love for us. Prior to His leaving earth to return to the Father, He wished to leave a living sign of that unique union in love. To accomplish this, He took the state of marriage, which the Book of Genesis tells us He had created, and raised it to the level of a sacrament so that a man and a woman united in married love could be a living sign of His love for all humankind by their living that love for each other wholeheartedly and sacrificially.

Finally, the Lord wanted human agents to celebrate and confer these sacraments so He called and ordained the Apostles and their successors to the priesthood. To them was given the power to renew His Passion, Death, and Resurrection, to infuse the life of grace through Baptism and strengthen it through Confirmation, to forgive sins, to anoint the sick and dying, and to witness marriage unions. The sacraments, then, are truly signs of Jesus continuing to minister to His People in today's world, seven amazing gifts. But there is more!

CHAPTER 7

On Becoming
the Sacraments

Too seldom do we think of what the sacraments require of us. We think only of our *receiving* them and thereby being the beneficiary of God's divine love. However, there is another whole dimension to the sacraments that we often overlook, and that is *becoming* the sacrament. Yes, it is not enough for us to *receive* these signs of God's mercy and love; we must then actually *become* those signs. For example, when we celebrate the Sacrament of Penance, through God's infinite mercy our sins are forgiven. However, if we are truly to celebrate that mercy in its fullness, then we must share it by becoming signs of forgiveness ourselves. How? By forgiving one another, especially those whom it is difficult to forgive. That can be hard, especially if someone, perhaps someone close to us, has hurt us seriously either in word or deed. Nonetheless, we are to forgive that person just as we have been forgiven. Recall Jesus' story of the unjust steward. Having been forgiven a huge debt, he refused to forgive a fellow servant a much smaller debt and for this he himself was severely punished.

The hallmark of a Catholic Christian is the virtue of forgiveness, a virtue too often lacking in our public lives. That's why the public is stunned when some Christian parent, whose child has been seriously injured or even killed, forgives the perpetrator. Consider the manner in which the Amish people in Pennsylvania not only forgave the person who took the lives of five of their children but even welcomed his family to their table. And recall the manner in which Pope John Paul II publicly forgave the man who attempted to assassinate him. On a human level, both theses actions seem absurd, but in God's plan, it is how we become living signs of Him who so readily forgave us by dying for us. Did He not teach us to pray, "Forgive us our trespasses *as we forgive those who trespass against us*"? In effect, Jesus is making our willingness to forgive others a qualification for Him to forgive us. The grace of the Sacrament of Penance both inspires and enables us to do so.

Consider the Sacrament of Confirmation which is given to strengthen us so that we will practice the very virtues we received in Baptism. As we noted above, it is actually our Baptism that is confirmed. Why? So we can be the person that He called us to be in that baptism. As we grow older, it becomes more difficult to practice those virtues so He confirms their role in our lives with the special sacramental grace of His Holy Spirit. Confirmation cannot be merely a sign that we are growing up, some kind of Christian Rite of Passage. It is much, much more. It is the source of the strength we will need to live a Catholic life in an increasingly secular and individualistic world. Too often do we ignore or not use those Confirmation graces, choosing instead to act as if the moral virtues by which we are called to live do not even exist. Rather, we are anointed to become the sacrament by responding to the inspiration of the Holy Spirit and thereby serve as a living sign of the values and virtues by which the Lord wishes us to live. In that way, the effects of our Baptism are strengthened to enable us to live so as to have others see Jesus living and working in and through us by practicing positive peer pressure.

A final example of becoming the sacrament involves an elderly woman who was nearing death. Summoned to her home, I found her in bed and her five teenage granddaughters sitting on the floor around her bed. They were weeping because their beloved grandmother was soon to die. I began the prayers and rites of the Sacrament of the Anointing of the Sick, asking them to leave the room for a few moments so I could hear the woman's Confession. When they returned, they joined in the litanies and beautiful prayers that accompany the anointing and then the reception of Holy Communion.

When the rites were concluded, the woman radiated that peace that comes with knowing that she was prepared to meet her Lord and, especially in her case, the Blessed Mother. The peace that she felt was radiated to those five granddaughters. Their tears were gone and they shared in their grandmother's inner healing and peace. I saw it continue to embrace them during the wake and Mass of Christian Burial. Through the special grace of the Sacrament of Anointing, their grandmother had *become* the sacrament and her actions transformed them. Along with and through their grandmother, they, too, had been healed.

We have reviewed all of the above to show the depth of meaning behind the sacraments of the Church, those signs of Jesus through which He still ministers to His people in today's world, providing us with the divine grace required for all of us to become living signs of His presence. Being those signs is an essential part of our response to His call to follow Him.

By God's design, it is the priest who is the primary channel of God's sacramental graces. It is he who acts in the person of Christ. It is he who is the principal instrument by which we are incorporated into Christ and through whom we are strengthened to respond to the circumstances of our daily life as God would have us respond. So it is through the priest, using the sacramental signs (water, bread, wine, oil, words) to signify sacramental graces he is administering, that the divine life of God is infused, sins are forgiven, virtues are strengthened, the sick are at least inwardly healed, marriage covenants are sanctified, and most importantly, Christ is made present, offered and received in the Eucharistic sacrifice. These actions bring with them a great responsibility for the priest himself to be an outstanding sign of Jesus to those whom he serves.

Again, the priest does not possess these powers because he deserves them. No man is worthy of being a priest. Therefore, we can conclude that it is through the powers of the Sacrament of Priesthood that he becomes the recipient of special sacramental graces which inspire and energize him to live as close to the example of Jesus as he can and to serve as the channel through whom Jesus confers His divine life. In these sacred actions he becomes a Sign of Christ in today's world.

CHAPTER 8

The Priest
as Priest

This chapter heading may seem strange following all we have said about the role of the priest in celebrating the sacraments. After all, isn't he a priest when he performs any and all of those rites? Of course, but what lies behind his actions? Where does he receive his inspiration, his energy, his ability to focus on the essentials of his ministry and not get caught up in distractions, self-centeredness or pride? The source is, of course, Jesus, the great High Priest and the channel for those graces is the priest's prayer life. Primarily, then, the priest must be a man of prayer for it is through a prayer relationship with the Lord that Jesus fashions the man into the channel of grace that He wants His priest to be. It is through daily prayer, if possible in the presence of the Blessed Sacrament, that the priest grows in his relationship with Jesus and allows himself to be formed more and more into the image of Christ. It is through heart to heart communication with the great High Priest, in whose priesthood he shares, that the priest opens himself daily to know the will of his Lord and to receive the graces necessary to carry out His will, especially when it is difficult or even contrary to his own.

·   Each day the priest needs the Lord's guidance in giving comfort and confidence to an aging parishioner, in finding the right words to strengthen the sick and the dying and their families, in being a source of faith and hope to those who mourn the loss of a loved one, in calming the distraught or angry and in offering direction to a penitent or someone seeking spiritual guidance. He needs compassion when guiding a woman and the father of the child in an unplanned pregnancy or helping a couple through a difficult marriage problem; when consoling the parents of a critically ill child or when encouraging young people to practice their faith in the face of negative peer pressure. He needs the Lord's inspiration to be patient with the complaining parishioner, and wisdom when making decisions about his parish. He needs fairness when working with his staff so as to treat them all equally, courage and honesty when approaching his parishioners for financial support for their parish, and good judgment when encountering those who come to the rectory seeking financial help. He needs patience and understanding when guiding younger priests in their formation, and daily he needs the Lord's encouragement so that he celebrates the sacraments with attention, devotion and a growing appreciation of how unworthy he is to do any and all of the above.

While this daily prayer is an essential source of inspiration and guidance from Father, Son and Holy Spirit, all of those actions spring from his fundamental role as one called to proclaim the Word and to offer the Sacrifice of the Mass, the principal reasons for his being called to the service of Christ's Mystical Body. It is in the Sacrament and Sacrifice of the Holy Eucharist, the one we call the Most Blessed Sacrament, where the priest most significantly acts in the person of Christ.

In every world culture, where there is someone designated

to be the priest, his principal function will be offering a sacrifice and leading his community in worship. Sometimes it is through specific designation, sometimes because he descends from a family of priests, as was the case of the Levitical priesthood of the Old Testament. Whatever the source and culture, it has always been the principal role of a priest to offer sacrifice. Nowhere is this more clearly evident than in the celebration of the Holy Sacrifice of the Mass.

Think about what it means to be the priest at the Mass. To begin, he has gone through a four to six year course of study on post-graduate level in order to prepare to be ordained. His courses will be demanding and serve him well as he learns to think in terms in which he probably has not thought before. There will be courses in Philosophy, Dogmatic Theology (the official teachings of the Church) along with Moral Theology which will deal with the Ten Commandments and the Precepts of the Church, Fundamental Psychology and how they all apply to today's living. In addition, he will study the Sacred Scriptures, Church Law and History, Liturgy, Homiletics, and other allied subjects. In today's Church his studies may also include learning a second language. How long all this training will take will differ depending on the diocese and/or religious order for which he is preparing and his previous academic studies.

During his time of formation, he will have reflected on the call he feels he has received from God. From time to time, he will have probably questioned whether that call is authentic, and through prayer, retreats and personal spiritual direction he will have concluded that his vocation is to serve God in the priesthood. If he has never worked full time in the business world, he probably will have been employed during his summer vacations and should have learned several things: how hard it is to make a living in this world, how to interact with female as well as male co-workers, how to deal with unpleasant assignments and demanding bosses, how to keep his spiritual life alive by consistently making time for daily Mass, meditation and for personal prayer and reflection, and other aspects of life in the busy world that will challenge him, perhaps even more after ordination. If he has already been in the professional world, then it is presumed that the skills thus attained will accompany him into his priesthood.

Once ordained, he will discover what the priesthood is *really* all about! So it is with any level of endeavor. All the study, prayer and other preparation provides a necessary and valuable foundation upon which to build but until those things are put into daily practice, they never really come alive. But that is what the second part of this book is about, so let's get back to the Mass.

The role of the priest in the Mass is two-fold. He is to proclaim and preach the Word of God and then he is to offer the Eucharistic Sacrifice. What awesome tasks these are! To proclaim the Word means more than reading it. It means studying it in private, prayerfully meditating on it, referring to Scripture commentaries for in-depth understanding of the text, determining which of the ideas his reflection produces should be the focus of his homily, and then—and this is *so* important—considering how he will suggest to his listeners how to apply those teachings to their daily life. The faithful come to be fed and inspired, not just to be taught. They want to take away at least one idea that they can work on that week; otherwise, the homily becomes simply a Scripture lesson.

In preparation for this task, the priest may start reading the Scriptures assigned for the following Sunday on the previous

Monday or Tuesday, opening himself in prayer to the promptings of the Holy Spirit who will help him to see applications for the Readings during the rest of the week. Or he might meet with a group of parishioners to read and share their faith-based reflections on the Readings and thereby draw from his parishioners some applications he might not have otherwise considered. In his earliest days of ministry, he might even preach his homily to someone who can help him with his delivery, perhaps a Speech or English teacher in his parish. Too many times have well thought out, well written and potentially powerful homilies missed their target because they were poorly, even boringly delivered. Further, there must be genuine fervor and faith evident in the delivery—this can't be faked—if the homilist is to stir up the faith of his listeners. Different priests will highlight different sections, quotes or ideas culled from the Readings, so there will be a different homily from each priest who ponders the Readings. Some of that will be fostered by the commentaries he reads, the personal experiences he has had, the "theologizing" he has done over the years, the connection he has with his parishioners and their personal or family lives, the specific needs of his parish or neighborhood as he has gotten to know them, and sometimes even where he himself is in his own personal development.

My mentor with whom I served as an associate pastor and who was my confessor for the last twenty years of his life, used to say, "Remember, sometimes when they preach, many priests are preaching to themselves," meaning that their homilies reflect where they are in their own spiritual lives. I'm sure it is not uncommon for many a priest, having completed his homily, to sit down in the Celebrant's Chair and say to himself, "Okay, now you do what you just told them to do!" I know that I've done it many times.

Following the homily, there comes the most awesome of all experiences for the priest, the celebration of the Liturgy of the Eucharist and all that it contains and accomplishes. It has often been said that the most important thing any Catholic can do on any day in their lives is to offer the Sacrifice of the Mass. Indeed, the most important thing the Holy Father does every day is celebrate Mass. Why? Quite simply, because it is the re-presentation, under the appearances of bread and wine, of the Passion, Death, Resurrection and Ascension of Jesus, the most important series of events in the history of the world. It is the gift given to His Church at the Last Supper which therefore places us believers in the most direct connection with the Lord Himself that we can experience on this earth.

As the Baltimore Catechism used to express it, "The Mass is the unbloody sacrifice of Calvary renewed." That is a mystery that we must reflect on over and over again, not so that someday we will understand it, because we never will, but because every effort made in that direction brings us a little bit closer to appreciating the unlimited mercy of God and His unconditional love for each of us as revealed in the Eucharist. Because the belief that Jesus is truly present under the appearances of bread and wine is a mystery, we must repeat it over and over, reflect on it over and over, teach it over and over, so that, with the help of God's grace and especially the unique sacramental graces of the Holy Eucharist, we can come to a deeper, but never complete, understanding of this extraordinary Gift of God.

Perhaps I can best illustrate this mystery, this joyous teaching of the Catholic Faith, with a true story. In the year 1997, I made a pilgrimage to the Holy Land with a group of my parishioners. It was the occasion of the Centennial Celebration of our parish and we felt there was no better way to celebrate that event. We had a wonderful guide, a young man who was a Syriac Catholic, who grew up in Jerusalem, really knew his way around and was able to get us little extra "bonuses" along the way, that is, unusual sights and special places to visit not ordinarily included on tours. As we approached the village of Nazareth, the home of the Holy Family, he told me that he had arranged for us to offer our daily Mass in the beautiful Basilica of the Annunciation.

Having been there once before, I assumed that we would use one of the side altars. I went to the sacristy to vest and then he said, "Please follow me." To my surprise, he led me to the main altar of the basilica—it is situated in a lower rotunda—and as I approached the altar to begin the Mass, I spotted a large bronze disc in the floor. On it were inscribed the words, *Hic Verbum Caro Factum Est.* They mean, "Here the Word was made flesh." I stopped dead in my tracks as the thought came to me: "This is where the angel told Mary that she was to be the mother of the Savior." But that was not all, for my next thought was: "In a sacramental way, I am about to experience what Mary did. By the power of the Holy Spirit which I received in my ordination, I am about to make Jesus present right here on this altar which stands in the place where He became our incarnate God. He will be just as truly present here as He was in the womb of the Virgin Mary." Moreover, because there was no major feast that day, the Readings were from the Mass of the Feast of the Annunciation, including St. Luke's beautiful telling of that earth-shaking event. So with those truly awesome thoughts running through my head and my heart, I began the celebration.

The homily I delivered was quite brief because, more eloquently than I ever could, the place and the event it honored spoke clearly for themselves. I began the preparation of the gifts and then moved into the Eucharistic Prayer, the Consecration, the Great Amen, the Lord's Prayer and Holy Communion. As I gave Holy Communion to my fellow pilgrims, many of them were in tears and when the Mass was over, one of them said to me, "I don't know where you were during the Eucharistic Prayer but you weren't with us."

Never had I so strongly felt the impact of the divine mystery that God has privileged me to make present as I did that day, and I can honestly say that I have never celebrated Mass since that time without being able to focus on precisely what I was doing, namely, changing the bread and wine into Jesus, the Son of God and our Savior, the Crucified and Risen Lord, the Great High Priest and our Brother. It is a grace I will cherish forever. It gives deeper meaning to those powerful words we were taught to say as children at the elevation of the Bread and Wine, "My Lord and My God!" How very true they are!

Clearly there is no greater privilege that can be given to a man than to say the words, "This is My Body," and "This is My Blood." They are the words of Jesus and, for reasons known only to Him, He has given this power to His priests, not a single one of whom is in any way worthy to even claim that privilege, but nonetheless is called to exercise it on behalf of God's People. This miraculous change is truly "the Mystery of our Faith" and in speaking those words and bringing about that change of the elements into Jesus the Lord, the priest truly, in the highest sense of the words, acts as another Christ.

There are so many ways we can try to express this most profound of all mysteries. For example, an old spiritual-style song, "He's Got the Whole World in His Hands" could well be sung about the priest at the moment of the Consecration because he does hold in his hands the Creator of all things. We can think about the words of the synagogue leader who came to ask Jesus to cure his servant and, when Jesus challenged his faith, responded, "Lord, I do believe; help my unbelief," words that many priests pray immediately following the Consecration. There is the reality that when I look at the Host now consecrated or at the Host in the monstrance exposed for our adoration, I am experiencing the closest we mere mortals can come to a face-to-face encounter with the Lord Jesus in this life. Further, when the priest is in adoration of the Blessed Sacrament, he has the additional realization that the Lord Jesus made Himself truly present in the consecrated Host through the actions and words of the priest himself. Is there any wonder, then, why I have come to the conclusion that the most amazing words in the New Testament, at least to me personally, are those that Jesus spoke at the Last Supper when He said to His new priests, "Do this in my memory"? He could have intended them for the Apostles alone so they would be fortified for the events of the next three days, but He intended that power to be passed on, as it has been for almost two thousand years, to the Catholic priests of every age. Surely, no greater gift can be given to a man.

Following the Consecration and the Great Amen by which the assembly declares its belief in and affirmation to what has just taken place, the priest has the added privilege of nourishing himself on his Savior, Jesus, now sacramentally present. It is a time for him to pause, at least for a few moments, to reflect on what he has just done: make Jesus present on the altar and then receive Him as his Food! That privilege is further extended when he calls his people to the table of the Lord and feeds his flock on the Body and Blood of Jesus whom he himself has made present. He thereby becomes, through Jesus, the binding force which unites with one another all those who receive their

Eucharistic Lord, the fundamental meaning of "Communion." Yes, the people are united individually to Christ but they are also united in the "one bread and the one cup" to one another, thereby becoming one body, the Mystical Body of Christ that is truly the Church.

For a further insight into this wondrous event, the Mystery of our Faith, let us reflect for a moment on the Thirteenth Station of the Cross in which the body of Jesus is placed into the arms of His mother. We are confronted with a remarkable scene. The mother of the Savior holds the dead body of her Son, ready but reluctant to turn it over to those who would bury Him. Now, in contrast, consider what happens at the Mass. Jesus has been offered once again to the Father in atonement for our sins and then, wonder of wonders, He is given to us as our Food! It is not the dead body given to Mary but the resurrected and triumphant Jesus, the Son of God, now living eternally with the Father, yet truly present among us, who is offered for us and to us. How extraordinarily great a Gift is that which we are given! And still there is more!

During the Mass we pray in union with the whole Church throughout the world and with all those who have gone before us in heaven and purgatory. In this way, the community of receivers goes beyond the limits of earth to include all faithful souls everywhere, and the priest at the altar is the human agent through whom the Lord accomplishes this miraculous union. Finally, at the conclusion of the Mass, it is the priest (or deacon) who sends the people forth to make the Mass a reality in their daily lives, urging them to carry out, to the best of their ability, the one commandment that Jesus gave us at the Last Supper, "Love one another as I have loved you." Surely there is no greater sign of God's love than the Mass they have just celebrated, for it is the renewal of His redemptive Sacrifice and His Resurrection.

So as our chapter title says, this is when the priest is most a priest, one with Christ in the eternal Sacrifice of the Son to the Father through the power of the Holy Spirit, because none of this could happen without the unique, awesome, eternal power bestowed by God upon His priest.

CHAPTER 9

The Priest at Prayer

When we spoke in a previous chapter of the requirements for a vocation to the priesthood, we listed as one of them a solid spiritual life. That would include spiritual reading, an exercise by which the person is steadily opened to the thoughts and inspirations of the great spiritual writers of the Church. It would also include devotional prayers such as the Rosary of Our Lady, the Stations of the Cross, special novenas, prayers to a particular favorite saint and so on. However, at the root of all of these is the person's personal prayer which constitutes an absolute essential for growth in his response to God's call to serve. If this is true of every baptized Christian, how much more true is it for the Catholic priest. He should be identified as "a man of prayer."

Prayer has often been defined as raising the mind and heart to God or carrying on a conversation with God. Moreover, while it may be supported and fed by the formal kinds of prayer just mentioned, this kind of prayer is that which springs directly from the heart of the person and is expressed in his or her own words. It is this kind of prayer that moves one beyond "saying prayers" or "reciting prayers," something we have done since we were children, to actually entering into a personal one-on-one dialogue with the Almighty. As one writer has expressed it, it is "one heart speaking to another Heart."

If the priest is to be a "stand-in" for God, then it is primarily through prayer that he acknowledges his total dependence upon God for the inspiration, grace, stamina and humility necessary to do His work and to do it well. If it is God's work that he is called to do, then he must daily acknowledge his human inadequacies and go to the Lord each day to obtain whatever will be necessary that day to complete his tasks in a priestly and fruitful manner. Nor can his daily celebration of the Mass be enough, as magnificent as that great prayer surely is. As one priest has stated it, "We cannot get so involved in the works of God that we forget the God whose work we do." A priest will probably experience spiritual dryness and even burnout before his time because he has become so busy that he has not taken time to pray, to keep in touch with the God who has called him to priesthood in the first pace.

It is essential that the parish priest be a man of personal prayer on a regular, that is, daily basis. This daily prayer is greatly enhanced when done in the presence of the Blessed Sacrament. It is here, following his morning Mass, perhaps late at night when locking up the church or some other time during the day that the parish priest comes face to face with the Great High Priest in whose priesthood he has been called to share. Here, truly, heart speaks to Heart.

For all who endeavor to pray, the most common type of prayer is the prayer of petition. Most people find it quite easy. Springing from our perceived needs or when we are in some kind of trouble, we turn to God for help and/or guidance and it is good for us to do so. Such prayer is of considerable value since it acknowledges our own weakness and brings us before God, begging His divine assistance and strength. It is in such prayer that we admit our dependence on God for all we need in order to know His will and carry it out. It is significant that the prayer that Jesus taught us, the Our Father, is composed of seven petitions. Reflecting on the Our Father provides us with the insight that all things come from the Lord and we are completely dependent upon Him for each of them. No matter what we feel we have accomplished in our lives, we come to realize that it is all in response to a constant flow of graces, gifts, circumstances and opportunities that He provides.

In this category of prayer of petition should be included the prayer of discernment, that is, trying to reach the right decision when a life decision needs to be made. For example, having been a high school teacher for twelve years and with the Second Vatican Council having occurred during that time, I began to feel that the new life of the Church was passing me by. My original intent was to be a parish priest and I felt the urge to return to parish ministry. Following a difficult first year, my teaching experience had been very positive and I had come to appreciate the influence that a priest/teacher can have on his students, so I brought the quandary to prayer. In that process and over a period of months, I came to the conclusion that the Lord wanted me to return to parish life but I also reflected on my growing awareness that I was not gifted where foreign languages were concerned. So having discerned that I should return to parish ministry, I also suggested to the newly formed Priest Personnel Board that I should not be assigned to an inner-city parish where a fluency in Spanish would make for a more fruitful ministry. Putting myself in their hands, I was assigned to a suburban parish where, in the next ten years, I served three remarkably gifted pastors who made a significant impact on my development as a parish priest and, ultimately, as a pastor.

The same process was called into play toward the end of my time as pastor in the last parish in which I served. Having been there for twenty years and having accomplished a number of good things with the help of the other priests, the staff and the laity, I began to understand the term "burn out." I was seven months away from my 75th birthday and the completion of my 49th year of ministry and wondered whether I should leave on that birthday or wait until my 50th Anniversary. Again I brought that decision to prayer, especially before our Eucharistic Lord, and, after a period of a few months, the answer came in my heart and from three very trusted friends. So it was that I retired on my 75th birthday and did so with a great deal of gratitude and inner peace. I have never looked back... but I did return to the parish to celebrate that 50th Anniversary!

In addition to the prayer of petition, there are three other forms of prayer that are called for in the life of anyone who is seeking to know God more intimately, whether it is said by a priest, religious or lay person.

The first of these is the prayer of sorrow or contrition. Here we acknowledge that we truly are sinful people who must regularly seek the forgiveness of our eternally loving God, not just out of fear of being punished but, even more importantly, out of the realization that, frail and finite mortals that we are, we have failed in our efforts to love our God who is the Source of everything that is good. In such prayer we sincerely admit that we are sinners, seek the Lord's forgiveness, renew our efforts to try to be more faithful, and beg His ongoing outpouring of grace to strengthen us in our resolve.

If this kind of prayer is required of everyone, how much more is it required of the priest. He who has been privileged to be a channel of God's forgiveness through his celebration of the Sacrament of Penance, must first of all personally acknowledge his own sinfulness and beg God's forgiveness and ongoing assistance to resist future temptation. Indeed, before they enter the Confessional or Room of Reconciliation to hear and absolve the sins of others, many priests pray a sincere Act of Contrition for themselves, thereby calling to mind their own weakness, while asking God for the wisdom and compassion to be the best possible instrument of His forgiveness towards those who come for absolution.

Moreover, if he is honest with himself, he will fully understand that, in light of the amazing power that God has given him, the power to forgive sins in God's holy name, he will conscientiously make regular use of the Sacrament of Penance himself. Moreover, in order to have his confessions result in steady growth, he will be wise to find a regular confessor who will get to know him and his soul and act as a spiritual director as well as the one who forgives his sins. On a personal note, when my regular confessor died, I felt like I had lost my anchor until, having gone to a number of different priests, I finally found another who would get to know me and be of real assistance in my efforts to grow.

Therefore, when he begins the celebration of the Eucharist, the celebrant will attentively participate in the Penitential Rite, including himself in the prayer, "May almighty God have mercy on us, forgive us our sins and bring us to everlasting life." The priest knows he is truly a "wounded healer" and is just as much in need of God's patience, mercy and forgiveness as anyone else who claims to be a follower of Jesus Christ. Moreover, isn't he about to offer the greatest act of atonement for sin that we have?

Another form of prayer is that of thanksgiving. Indeed, it is thanksgiving that lies at the very heart of the Mass, for the word "Eucharist" means "thanksgiving." Do we not declare, "It is right to give Him thanks and praise" at the beginning of the Eucharistic Prayer? And so it is. While being another form of recognition that we depend on God for everything that is good, expressions of thanksgiving are too often in short supply in our prayer life. We are very good at asking for what we need (the prayer of petition), but how often do we spend time and effort expressing our thanks to God when He grants what we have asked for? As children, we learned that "Thank You" was one of those "magic words" we were all supposed to use, yet it too often is overlooked in our prayer life. Nor do we have to have something specific for which to express our thanks. It is incumbent on us to develop an ongoing attitude of gratitude which will allow us to grow daily in our appreciation of the constant outpouring of graces and the multitude of other good gifts He bestows on us. Those gifts include our parents and grandparents, brothers and sisters and other relatives, close friends, priests, deacons, religious brothers and sisters, teachers, coaches, mentors, as well as life's opportunities, health, talents and aptitudes, sunrises and sunsets, the whole array of nature's beauties and marvels, and even all the challenges that come from the Lord throughout every moment of every day, for it is through them that we grow. Nor should we ever forget that not one single gift that God grants us is in any way deserved! They result entirely from the outpouring of His divine love. Indeed, from the very first moment that our heart beats in our mother's womb, we are increasingly indebted to God for the constancy of His goodness.

If all the above is to be developed in anyone claiming to be a follower of Christ, how much more is it expected of the priest, the "other Christ"! Daily prayer, both formal and personal, must be the foundation on which he builds his spiritual life so that it is strong enough to support not only himself but all those for whom he is called upon to pray and to provide loving service.

Nor should we overlook the prayer of acceptance. From time to time, when bad things happen, we all are inclined to ask, "Why me, Lord?" Should we not also ask, "Why me, Lord?" about all those wonderfully *good* things that God grants us each day? Is there anything that we have or experience that we do not receive?

As for those who complain that God did not answer their prayers, we would affirm that God does answer all prayers in one of three ways. He says, "Yes" or He says, "Keep asking" (perhaps to test our perseverance), or He says, "I have a better idea!" It may seem as though He is saying, "No" but then, if we are attentive in our prayer, He will reveal to us a better path than the one we asked for because only He truly knows what is best for us. However He answers our prayers, it becomes increasingly clearer as we grow older that He always does respond, perhaps not as we wish but by bestowing what we come to realize over time is the best possible answer. So it is that, in time, we learn to trust Him. After all, He is God! How much we would benefit and how more swiftly would we grow if, at the beginning of each day, we could say and truly mean, *Lord, help me to remember that nothing can happen to me today which You and I together can't handle.*

The final form of prayer is that of adoration, a form that many find difficult or simply don't think of, yet it is traditionally the first form of prayer that the spiritual writers encourage us to practice. We find good examples of it in such prayers as the "Glory to God" which we say at Mass, in prayers to be said in the presence of the Blessed Sacrament, in many of the psalms, in reflecting on the lives of the saints. The "Wow!" of a beautiful sunrise or sunset, an awesome wonder of nature such as the Grand Canyon, Niagara Falls, the heavens on a crystal clear night, the birth of a child, a newborn animal, an outstanding performance of classical music composition, a miraculous cure and the wisdom of a child can all bring us to true adoration if we are open to it. There are so many things happening all around us that should lead us to prayer of adoration if only we attune ourselves to them.

By the very nature of his calling, all of these forms are to be prominent in the life of a priest. He is often defined as "a man of prayer" and rightly so, for he is to be the primary intercessor on earth for his community as well as an example of the other forms of prayer treated above. Clearly, he is the one through whom his people reach out to God in every celebration of the Mass where, as we have seen, he is another Christ. It is he who proclaims the Word and explains and applies it, who prepares the gifts of bread and wine and then, by the power of the Holy Spirit, changes them into the Body and Blood of the Lord Jesus. It is he who then offers Christ, now sacramentally present, to the Father, and finally, the one who feeds his people with their Eucharistic Lord. What a truly awesome role this is! The word "awesome" is terribly overused today but, in its true meaning of generating a sense of awe and wonder in someone or something, it is accurately used in this context. Together with the people, the priest, in his role as presider at the Mass, prays, "Lord, I am not worthy," with a meaning that is over and above that of the people, for he is truly acting in the place of God and using what can only be described as divine powers, a gift of which he is absolutely unworthy. This kind of prayerful awareness keeps him grounded and humbled even as he handles these divine elements.

All the above presume a development over time in the practice of meditation or, even deeper, contemplation. The term "meditation" frightens some people as they think this form of prayer is reserved to priests and monks and brothers and nuns. Actually, if you can think, you can meditate! For example, reading a passage from the Scriptures and then thinking about how you can apply that to your life, or how it fits into the larger context in which it is found, or how the people in Jesus' time reacted to it, or even just dwelling on the scene and placing yourself in it are all ways in which one can meditate. It is through this practice that we are drawn by the Holy Spirit into a deeper relationship with the Father, Son and Holy Spirit and open the way for them to be more active in our lives and for us to be more responsive to their presence. It is a kind of prayer which, over time, will strengthen us in faith, hope and love and all the other virtues which can bear much spiritual fruit each day. It is through meditation that we learn to walk with Christ in all the events of our lives as we grow in faith, in compassion, in generosity, and in steadfastness in time of trial.

The Liturgy of the Hours, sometimes called the Divine Office, is another form of prayer that is required of the priest. It is a responsibility taken on when one is ordained to the diaconate and which mandates that he use the Hours for part of his daily prayer, and the obligation continues until it can no longer be fulfilled. In the busy life of a parish priest, it serves to provide an instrument of prayer which guarantees that, at least some time in the priest's day, he will step aside from his demanding duties and spend time conversing with God. While it is a formal and required means of prayer, it is nonetheless a great source of strength, comfort, hope and praise which, when devoutly prayed, can greatly enhance and enrich the priest's own life. Because it contains prayers of praise for God's many deeds, contrition for our sins coupled with hope for forgiveness, petition for the graces needed to continue the struggle to live each day in God's will, thanksgiving for the continuing divine generosity of God in spite of ourselves, seeking protection from our enemies and justification for our actions, and other aspects of our relationship with the Lord, it can be seen to be a great source of developing a growing intimacy with Him. But there is more.

When we examine the Liturgy of the Hours we find that it is essentially a book of Psalms to which have been added selections from the rest of the Scriptures, readings from the Fathers and Church Documents, as well as canticles, i.e., special songs from the Gospels. The canticles are three: (1) the *Benedictus* which is the song of praise sung by Zechariah at the birth of his son, John the Baptist, (2) the *Magnificat* which is the song of praise sung by the Virgin Mary during her visit with Elizabeth, and (3) the *Nunc Dimittis* which is a song of thanksgiving sung by Simeon at the Presentation of the Lord in the Temple.

Because these psalms are so ancient—at least two centuries before Christ—and were such a part of the life of the devout Jew at Jesus' time, they are the prayers which Jesus Himself prayed in the synagogue and temple and at other times. In the Gospels He quotes from them from time to time. As a result, the psalms bring us into direct contact with Jesus since, in praying or singing them, we pray or sing the very prayers He used each day. Since priests stand in the place of Jesus before His People, this is only fitting and proper.

In addition, because the praying of the Liturgy of the Hours is required of every ordained minister throughout the world, the priest is put into a special connection with all his brother priests through these prayers. To achieve that end, the Liturgy of the Hours is divided into seven sections: Morning Prayer, Mid-Morning, Mid-Day and Mid-Afternoon Prayer, Evening Prayer, Night Prayer and Readings. Ideally, these are said at the times stipulated but, due to the uncertainty of the parish priest's schedule, sometimes two or three of these sections are prayed in one sitting. However, whenever they are prayed, they provide a great source of union and support rising from the knowledge that the same prayers being offered here and now are also being offered throughout the day and around the world, thus providing another very special bond of union in the priestly fraternity. In short, when the priest prays the Office, he knows that he is joining in prayer with his brothers in Christ throughout the world. What a great gift this is!

How heartening it is, too, to know that more and more lay persons have begun to pray the Divine Office either in private or with a group. Having had the personal experience of praying Morning Prayer with those attending a weekday Mass just prior to the celebration itself, I know from their testimony how much they enjoy and benefit from it and how well it prepares them for the celebration of the Mass.

CHAPTER 10

The Priest
as Celibate

To many people, Catholic and non-Catholic, one of the most puzzling aspects of the Catholic priesthood is the required promise or vow of celibacy. (The diocesan priest makes a promise; the religious order priest makes a vow.) Probably no other aspect of the parish priest's life has undergone such intense scrutiny in our time as has this one, and with good reason. In a culture that reveals diminishing concern about the pledge that couples make to a true commitment to a marital union that will last "all the days of my life," there are those who wonder why so much emphasis is placed on the practice of the Church that says her priests may not marry. When one considers a prevailing view of marriage as something that is "nice for those who want it" but which can be cast aside by those who do not, is it not understandable that some people feel that celibacy should be presented as only an *option* offered to the man who feels called to the priesthood? After all, the mandate to live a celibate life is a man-made law, not one laid down by Jesus, so why could it not be changed? And wouldn't such an option be a really fine remedy to the steadily decreasing number of men who feel called to the priesthood but have difficulty with the requirement of celibacy? Moreover, wouldn't a married priest be better equipped to counsel those members of his parish who are having marriage problems? And since it seems that God has called most men and women to the married state, isn't a celibate life somewhat unnatural in today's world? Further, isn't mandated celibacy one of the primary reasons behind the sex abuse scandal of recent years?

These and similar questions and their proposed single solution, namely, to allow priests to marry, seem to be good reasons for doing away with the life of celibacy required of the Catholic priest. However, when examined, most of them, if not all, reveal a poor understanding of precisely what celibacy is and why it currently is required for priesthood. So let's review what celibacy is really all about and, in doing so, endeavor to respond to the questions proposed above.

Celibacy can be defined as a state in life in which abstention from the use of one's sexual powers is required in order to foster single-minded devotion to God and faithful service to His people. It means that a man puts aside the right to marry and have a family in order to wholeheartedly give himself to the service of Jesus and His Church. It is a long-standing discipline in the Latin (Roman) Church which forbids marriage to priests and bishops and which normally excludes married men from ordination. While it continues to be the practice in some Eastern rite churches to allow a married person to be ordained, it should be noted that this practice is currently on a steady decline. Further, while a recent post-Vatican II pastoral provision allows Anglican priests who convert to Roman Catholicism to be ordained even if married, I recall one of these men, who was married with children and whom I was assisting in his preparation for ordination, saying to me, "I can never be the priest you are because of the obligation imposed on me to care for my family. Your celibacy has freed you for total service to God and His People."

We must remember that continence is expected to be practiced by *all* Catholic men and women as long as they are single, with God providing the grace to maintain this purity or chastity in every case. Essentially, then, a man who seeks entrance to the priesthood is basically being asked to continue to maintain that purity for the rest of his life, just as it is required for all men who do not marry. This teaching is often overlooked in today's society in which sexual activity is not only countenanced but almost expected on the part of all who are capable of it and where the loss of one's virginity is regarded almost as a rite of passage.

One of the happier trends we are witnessing among a growing number of our youth is the realization that their virginity is the most precious gift they can give to the person with whom they ultimately choose to spend the rest of their adult life. Please God, this trend will continue so that maintaining one's virginity until marriage or taking on a life of celibacy in the priesthood or religious life will no longer be regarded as somewhat unnatural, let alone abnormal or even bizarre.

Having said that, a brief review of the history of this practice in priesthood can begin when Jesus refers to such a life in Matthew's Gospel (19:10-12). After stating that adultery for either a man or woman is wrong, the disciples respond, *"If that is the case between man and wife, it is better not to marry." Jesus responded, "Not every one can accept this teaching, only those to whom it is given to do so. Some men are incapable of sexual activity from birth, some have been deliberately made so, and some there are who have freely renounced sex for the sake of God's reign. Let him accept this teaching who can."* Of course, there are those who blithely counter with an often proposed "fact," "But the Apostles were married," to which we can accurately respond that, even though there is the possibility of some of them being married, the fact is that we actually know from the Scriptures of only *one* Apostle who was married, Peter; and we know that fact only from the incident in which Jesus healed Peter's mother-in-law. Even in this case, there is no evidence that Peter's wife was still living at the time this incident took place. Jesus, the High Priest, Himself lived as a celibate and it is Jesus who is the model for all priests.

Were there married priests in the early days of the Church? Most likely there were but it was something that in a relatively brief time was gradually discontinued. Indeed, in his First Letter to the Corinthians, probably composed before Mark's Gospel which was written around 55-60 AD, St. Paul writes, *"I would like you to be free of all worries. The unmarried man is busy with the Lord's affairs and concerned with pleasing the Lord, but the married man is busy with the world's demands and occupied with pleasing his wife.... I have no desire to place restrictions on you but I do want to promote what is good, what will help you to devote yourselves entirely to the Lord."* (7:32-33, 35) We must also remember that the teachings and practices of the Church were not all presented in a nice tidy package from the very beginning. Indeed, the early Church was very often under persecution, so given that the Church was literally fighting for her life, matters that were doctrinal or disciplinary (as is celibacy) took time to be developed. Consider, for example, that the Feast of Christmas was not celebrated widely until the mid to late fourth century and not officially by the universal Church until the year 425 AD! Up to that time, all the emphasis was on the teaching and miracles of Jesus and, most importantly, on celebrating His Passion, Death, and Resurrection.

So the earliest formulation of this discipline of celibacy is found in the documents of the Council of Elvira (306 AD), with some recent evidence indicating that the discipline was possibly of apostolic authority. Subsequent Conciliar and papal documents reinforced this discipline in the Western Church. The uninterrupted discipline of celibacy, then, is at least fifteen hundred years old.

Why is it required? There are several reasons. The first is a corollary to the teaching that the priest is another Christ. Therefore, the priest should endeavor to live a celibate life just as Jesus did. In addition, by his call to minister to God's people in whatever way he can, he needs to be free of the concerns with which a married man (and father) is often preoccupied. He needs to be available to his people whenever and wherever they need him. He does not function just on weekends at Mass and hearing Confessions, visiting the sick or caring for the dying but in many other pastoral roles. He also needs to be free to spend time in prayer, conversing with his Lord while seeking to know His will and begging God's assistance in carrying out the many and varied aspects of his ministry. If there is a better definition of the current expression "24/7" than a truly dedicated parish priest, I have not encountered it.

What about the man who feels called to the priesthood but wishes also to be married? His first response must be to bring this dilemma to the Lord in prayer seeking assistance in responding to one or the other option. As we have seen, part of the reason for the several years of seminary training prior to ordination is to give a man sufficient time to help him to discern if God is actually calling him to priesthood. (Remember, it's a call, not a personal choice and surely not a right.) Since celibacy is "part of the package," he needs to seek the guidance of the

Holy Spirit and a spiritual director or guide in making this most important decision. Nor is this a once-and-it's-done decision like buying a house or joining a club. It is a decision which, through prayer and perseverance, calls for a frequent, perhaps even daily renewal of one's commitment just as is often true in a marriage relationship. For a number of men, celibacy is not an easy undertaking; indeed, it can sometimes be a lifelong struggle, but once embraced, the priest receives from God the grace of the Sacrament of Ordination, the divine power that he needs to be faithful to his promise. Then it is up to him to cooperate with that grace.

As for the noteworthy decline in priestly vocations in our country and others in the Western world, the simplistic solution of allowing priests to marry is really not a valid one. Permitting a married clergy brings with it a whole lot of other considerations. To name just a few, the married priest must, by his marriage vows, give his spouse the primacy of place when making important decisions. Further, if they have children there follow the daily and varied added responsibilities which would further reduce the priest's availability for service to the people of his parish. In addition, having one or more priests in a parish would necessitate that the parish provide double or triple the housing facilities as well as a considerable increase in the cost of maintaining two or more families while also securing each priest's family's future. In the event that the priest's marriage does not turn out to be a successful one and ends in divorce, such a circumstance would seriously compromise the priest's integrity when preparing couples for marriage or when called upon to provide marriage counseling, to say nothing of the possible scandal that would follow. And these are just a few of the challenges that having a married clergy would initiate.

It can also be pointed out that many of the Protestant sects are also experiencing a drop in vocations and they do permit their clergy to marry, so marriage is not a solution to any of the present problems facing the priesthood.

Is it possible that this rule of mandated celibacy could be changed in the future? The answer is Yes, because it is a man-made law, as we have seen, and therefore can be changed. The late John Cardinal O'Connor, in stressing the need for more men to become priests, frequently stated that without the priest there is no Eucharist and without the Eucharist there is no Catholic Church. One can argue, then, that because it is our belief in the Real Presence of Jesus in the Eucharist that sets us apart from almost all other Christian denominations, in order to be sure that there are sufficient priests to celebrate the Mass and share the Eucharistic Jesus with their people, there may come a time when married men can serve as priests for the greater good of the whole Church. Obviously, for this to take place, the Church would have to take a very long and penetrating look at its concept of priesthood and "think outside the box," a process that we will address about a different role in the chapter on "The Priest as Administrator." However, it is unlikely that modifying or doing away altogether with the promise of celibacy will occur in the near future and so we will continue as we are, hoping that those who are called will be moved by the Holy Spirit to freely and joyfully embrace the present requirement of celibacy.

In conclusion, then, the discipline of celibacy in the Catholic priesthood has been an essential part of priestly life in the Western Church for over fifteen hundred years. It has allowed countless thousands of priests to minister with singular, generous and tireless hearts to millions of people, both Catholic and non-Catholic, and they thereby have provided as best they could an image of an all-loving Jesus to their people. They have served as a living lesson to the secular world that celibacy can not only be lived but lived joyfully, and have sacrificed their right to marry and raise a family so that they can minister to all people, both single and married, in the name of Christ, the High Priest.

Having dealt with the basics of celibacy, we now ask, "How does the priest maintain his state of celibacy?" There are several ingredients that contribute to a successful endeavor. The first is a solid prayer life. If he is to be truly another Christ, then he must stay close to Jesus and the principal means of doing this is through his daily prayer, that is, staying in personal and intimate contact with the very Source and Inspiration of his call to the priesthood. To be a true image of Jesus he must stay close to Him and be strengthened by Him.

To take that idea a step higher, the Eucharist will serve as a great source of strength for maintaining the chastity that is required of the celibate. Not only by celebrating the mystery of Jesus' saving work as he does in each Mass, but also by receiving his Eucharistic Lord in each celebration, the priest shares in the greatest means given to us for maintaining the purity required of every follower of Jesus but especially of the priest. The practice followed by many of spending an hour each day before the Lord in His Eucharistic presence also provides that time away from the busyness of parish life. During this time the priest can bring his hopes and fears, his desires and failings, his challenges and decisions to the One who called him to share in His Priesthood, confident that the will of the Lord will be made known to him and he will receive the outpouring of strength he seeks to successfully and fruitfully respond to that call.

There is an added dimension to the Eucharistic Mystery that is unique to the priest. It springs from the role he plays when standing in for Christ the Priest, but goes deeper than offering the sacrifice and receiving his Lord in Holy Communion. It happens when he speaks the words of Consecration that change the bread and wine into the Body and Blood of Jesus. At that time, two things happen. First, he speaks in the first person the words of Jesus, thereby making them his own: "This is My Body, take and eat; this is My Blood, take and drink." These words primarily make the priest the instrument of God as he speaks in God's name, uttering His very own words and bringing about the sacramental change we call transubstantiation. At the same time, the priest, aware of the profundity of his words, can also apply them to himself, understanding that in doing so, he is offering *his* body and blood to the Father to be dedicated totally to the service of his Lord and His Church. Reflecting on this mystery from time to time reminds the priest of the consecration of his own body, of his own person that he offered to God on the day of his ordination to be used as God decides.

From another point of view, as the father of a family, besides the joy of bringing children into the world and seeing them grow into the persons he hopes them to become, a father also has to do things he would rather not but he does them because they are required as part of his vocation. It can be the same for a priest. As we will see in the second part of this book, he will have to do things he would rather not do but they are part of his calling so he endeavors to do them to the very best of his ability. Both biological and spiritual fatherhood call for sacrifices and it cannot be otherwise.

One of my classmates lived this approach in extraordinary fashion when, having been paralyzed from the waist down as the result of a surgical error, he spent the last fourteen years of his life in a hospital bed. Though physically able to say Mass only once or twice a week, he willingly accepted this cross every minute of his life during that period, dedicating his life to God's service in the only way he could. Truly, then, the words, "This is my body given for you" were lived out in a most graphic and grace-filed manner during the last years of his life.

One other important component of the priest's life and his promise and efforts to remain celibate is a strong devotion to the Blessed Virgin Mary. As the Mother of Jesus, she played a singular role in preparing Him for His ministry. Mary stands ever ready to obtain for her Son's priests all the graces they need to live their lives in a priestly manner. Every priest should pray every day for Mary to show her motherly care for her Son's priests and thereby rededicate himself each day to the service of her Son. The most powerful way for that to be done is through a faithful and reflective praying of her Rosary every day. On the Cross, Jesus gave Mary to John, one of His first priests. He also gave John to Mary, making her his mother and, by extension, the mother of all priests. Simply put, no priest can have a more powerful intercessor in Heaven than the Blessed Mother when she is called upon to assist and guide him in the varied aspects of his life and his ministry.

Besides a strong prayer life and a deepening understanding of his unique role in the celebration of the Sacrifice and Sacrament of the Eucharist, a regular celebration of the Sacrament of Penance serves as a solid source of that sacramental grace which is uniquely designed for the purpose of aiding the penitent by fortifying him against any inclination that could otherwise overcome his commitment. Regular use of Confession, together with the guidance of a strong spiritual director, is essential to combating temptation to violate one's promise. Connected with this wonderful sacrament is a firm effort to avoid any circumstances that would lead to sin. In a ministry that today brings the average parish priest into more frequent contact with women than ever before, he must be on his guard against developing relationships that would compromise his promise. Jesus must be the "significant other" in his life, the solution to any problem involving loneliness, the inspiration to keep going when the burden gets heavy, the source of strength needed to walk with the Lord who has promised to make his yoke easy and his burden light, together with seeking the strengthening brotherhood of his fellow priests.

There will also arise the need for human contact and the resulting gift of friendship. This can be found with his family, with lay persons who are well-grounded in their own spiritual lives, and with his brother priests. Toward this end, in recent years it has become the practice of a number of priests to gather weekly with others who share in their priesthood so as to bond with them in every aspect of their ministry. Such a priestly community serves well to reinforce each member in all that they are called upon to do and be. Programs such as *Jesus Caritas* serve this purpose in a very profitable way for all who are involved.

A regular period of exercise, recreation and attention to one's diet also provide a beneficial approach to combating fatigue and help greatly toward keeping a healthy attitude in mind and body so as to keep one's focus on his ultimate goal of being Christ to others.

All that has been said above should have provided answers to the questions asked at the beginning of this section, but there still remains that question which seeks an explanation to the steadily decreasing number of priestly vocations. The answers are several and, because some excellent books have been written responding to this question in greater depth and detail than this volume allows, it will be addressed here only in summary fashion and in no particular order of priority. Up until the 1970's and 1980's, the many sisters, brothers and priests who staffed our Catholic elementary and high schools were regular sources of encouragement to young men who gave any evidence of pursuing the priesthood. Their own example of dedication and commitment to the service of the Church was often the inspiration that resulted in their students considering whether God was calling them to priestly ministry or the religious life.

Sadly, their presence in our schools is now minimal at best because they, too, are experiencing a serious drop-off in vocations to the religious life, so this source of inspiration and support is no longer present. Some of the contributing factors were the reworking of the rules of the various communities which were problematic especially for the older members, the misreading of exactly what "the spirit of the Council" called for, the general attitude of "liberation" that took over whole segments of our society in the '70s and '80s, and the growing emphasis on self instead of one on others. (To suggest, by the way, that they, too, ought to be allowed to marry to solve *their* vocation shortage would, as we have seen, serve only to exacerbate their problems.)

The reality is that we Catholics do not live in a vacuum; we are just as open to being influenced by the culture in which we live as are so many others around us, and the culture active in today's society is, in large part, egocentric and humanistic. It focuses its attention on the individual as an individual and far less on that person's membership in the community to which they are at least partly responsible. Since the priesthood is essentially about spending oneself wholeheartedly through loving service to others in God's name, the current culture is clearly not conducive to producing people who are willing to live or even think about living such lives of sacrifice. Indeed, that word, "sacrifice," is not one we hear spoken very much today unless someone acts in some heroic way and is therefore seen to be an exception to the norm. In short, while we may admire it when it is encountered, sacrifice is no longer a motivating principle for a large number of people.

Even more influential in our daily lives is the heresy of consumerism which tells us that success in our lives will be measured by how much we make and how much we own. Remember the story told above of the father who put a price tag on the education of the priest? Our American society is preoccupied with the right car, the latest fashion, the most up-to-date electronic device, the size of the TV screen, the length, location and cost of the vacation, the membership in "the club," the "inherited" box seats at the professional sports event, the amount left in the will to one's survivors and other materialistic measurements; in short, "the bottom line." This atmosphere requires a man of considerable self-assurance and deep faith to put all that aside in order to live the relatively simple life of the parish priest when the pull in the opposite direction can be mighty strong.

As for arguing that being married would make a priest a better marriage counselor, would it not then follow that a doctor could not properly treat a seriously ill patient unless he had the same malady, or a therapist not properly counsel a patient unless he had experienced the same emotional problems? Hundreds of priests can testify that, precisely because they are *not* married, they have been privileged to share in the lives of many, many couples, both happily married and not so happily married, and were thereby able to offer truly objective and productive advice resulting from their education and vast experience not colored by their own singular relationship had they been married.

Finally, while no one would deny that even one case of sex abuse is one too many because of the severe damage that is done to the abused person, damage that may never be corrected, the recent sex abuse scandal in the Church in the United States has resulted in severe damage also to the image of the Catholic priesthood. How did it come about? Among several reasons, for too many years bishops and other authorities charged with the assignment of priests have endeavored to solve a priest's problem, whether it be sex abuse or alcohol or drug addiction, by reassigning him in the hope that a change in environment would be the answer. In some cases those priests were sent to existing facilities where they were treated for their problem, but sadly, in most cases, following recommendations by those professionals who did not know as much as they do now, their reassignment was seen to be the solution.

We know now that this method proved painfully, even disastrously ineffective. As a result, the U.S. Bishops' meeting in Dallas in 2004 sought to solve the problem by establishing a Safe Environment Program which requires a background check on all church employees and volunteers who deal in any way with children and it has proved to be quite successful. In addition, the dioceses of the country continue to educate their people on this matter through this well organized and ongoing Safe Environment Program.

It should be noted in this connection that the clergy sex abuse scandal, which severely tarnished the image of the parish priest, actually involved *less than 2%* of Catholic priests nationwide. Further, due to the resulting heightened national awareness by the public that the sexual abuse of children and teenagers is more widespread in our culture than was previously imagined, it has been determined through clear evidence that such abuse of children occurs far more often in public schools, on neighborhood teams, in other social groupings, and even within their own families. The facts show that there are many more abusers among the laity than among priests. Therefore, the notion that allowing priests to marry would solve the problem of sex abuse by the clergy is a shallow attempt to find a quick-fix to a much deeper problem. The media would much rather sensationally profile the "predator priest" than the local teacher or coach or family member who does not have the alleged "deep pockets" of the Church.

So it appears that sexual abuse is much more the result of the sex-obsessed culture in which we live than many would care to admit. Moreover, the realization that the majority of priests involved in the abuse cases were guilty of homosexual activity much more than child abuse indicates that this problem is surely not something that can be "cured" by entering into marriage.

One final thought on this subject. While being a priest currently denies a man the privilege of being a biological father, it does not deny his being a spiritual father. Indeed, "Father" is a title we very much cherish. It arises from our role as the channel through which the seed of the life of grace is planted in the soul of a person who is baptized. It is through the direct ministry of the priest that the planting of this divine seed—which will then be nourished by Mother Church through the Sacraments and the Mass—actually takes place. His is the initial act of giving life; it is the priest who fathers each baptized soul into the new life of grace. What a joy it is for him later on to meet a teenager or adult whom he has baptized and to be addressed by that person as "Father." What a significant role the priest has played in that person's life and how grateful he is to be able to carry out that role. Moreover, the priest is thereby sacramentally tied into the Fatherhood of God in a most unique manner and what an extraordinary privilege that is. It was one of the North American martyrs who declared that if he did only one baptism in his ministry before dying, it would have been worth all the preparation he had gone through. No wonder we rejoice in being called "Father"!

Chapter 11

The Priest and
the Sacraments

A s we have seen in Chapter 7, the Sacraments of the Church are the means instituted by Christ to continue His ministry to His People in today's world. They are seven signs of His continuing to pour forth His divine life, the life we call grace, upon all those who are open to it. They embrace the entire span of one's life thus bringing the recipient closer to God and more intimately connected with Him. Each one of these sacred signs brings with it a specific grace that enables the recipient to fulfill its purpose, and it is the priest who is the primary channel through which this grace is bestowed. Let us examine the priest's role in each of these sacramental celebrations.

The Sacrament of Baptism

In the parish in which I served as pastor for the twenty years before I retired from full-time parochial ministry, we were blessed to have two associate pastors as well as a priest who provided help on weekends. All four of us were necessary to properly serve the needs of the more than 4,700 registered families that made up our parish. One year, as we approached Lent and Holy Week, we were meeting with other staff members to plan the details of the various ceremonies which included the Lenten and Easter rituals that are part of the RCIA process. During the meeting, one of the other priests asked, "Do you think the priests could rotate the major celebrations of the Triduum (Holy Thursday, Good Friday and the Easter Vigil), so that over the next few years each of us could be the principal celebrant at each of them?" My response? "Sure! You three can rotate Holy Thursday and Good Friday but I will do Holy Saturday!"

That may sound presumptuous on my part but I tell that story to illustrate how important I feel that very special celebration is for the pastor, for those receiving sacraments for the first time and for the parish at large. There is no Mass that I enjoyed celebrating more than the Easter Vigil. Besides, given the early age at which pastors are now appointed, each of the other priests would soon get their turn to do the same. Nor should the enjoyment be the priest's alone. No Catholic should go through life without at least once having the exciting and uplifting experience of participating in this once-a-year glorious celebration of the Lord's Resurrection and our rising with Him. Having done it once, you will very likely return again and again.

Having made at least parts of the journey with the candidates and catechumens, I wanted to be the one who would ultimately baptize them, confirm them and give them their first Eucharist. Receiving their profession of faith, bringing them to the baptismal pool and then using my hands to pour the water over them, watching them step out of the pool soaking wet and with this huge smile on their face is one of the highlights of the year. Then giving them their white robe and finally their baptismal candle lit from the newly lit Paschal Candle, the sign of the resurrected Jesus, filled me with excitement and a renewed sense of what it is to be truly a life-giving father. It was giving them a rebirth into a whole new way of life and isn't that what Baptism really is all about?

"I have come that they may have life and have it to the fullest." "Go out, therefore, to all the nations and teach them what I have commanded you, baptizing them in the name of the Father and of the Son and of the Holy Spirit." In these two statements, Jesus declares the principal purpose of His coming among us. It was to undo the loss of eternal life that had resulted from the sin of Adam and Eve, our first parents, the sin we call "Original." It had been the plan of God to fashion humans as the crowning glory of His creation and to live in perfect harmony with them for all eternity. Sadly, by exercising their uniquely human gift of free will by an act of disobedience, they forfeited that future and introduced sin into the world. As a result, their sin affected not only the human race but, in fact, all of creation. Therefore, in addition to laying the ground work for our sins and those of others, whenever we encounter pain, suffering and death, war, famine, floods and other natural disasters, we are experiencing the disorder that sin brought into God's perfect world. This is the answer to "the problem of evil" that has intrigued the finest minds throughout the ages. Quite simply, whatever we would call evil in the world is the result of sin, both personal and generic. However, because God is pure love and would not allow His creation to be thus disordered forever, He sought to rectify it and restore to the human race, to nature and to the universe, that peace and order that He had planned and created in the first place. On the occasion of the fall of our first parents, He promised to send a Savior, quite literally a "Redeemer" who would "buy back" what had been lost. He sustained this hoped for redemption for centuries through promises and prophecies until that moment in time when He sent His own Son to be our Savior. "God so loved the world that He sent His only Son to save us." (John 3:16) So it was by the Passion, Death and Resurrection of Jesus that God's promise was fulfilled, our sins were forgiven, and the gates of heaven were once more opened for those who would be faithful to God's holy will.

Consider for a moment the statement that "our sins were forgiven." Were the question, "What is our principal goal in life?" posed today to older Catholics, many of them would respond, "To save our souls," for that is what they were taught. If they mean that they are to use the means provided by God to accept His gift of Faith and live accordingly, then they would have given a proper answer. However, there is a prior reality that must be understood if we are to make real in our lives the full meaning of the redeeming work of Jesus and the depth of the love His work revealed. It is this: Our souls have already been saved! That is what the whole Passion, Death and Resurrection were about! That saving work, as it is often called, is precisely that—the means whereby we were all saved from our sins and given the opportunity to share in the eternal life that God had originally planned for us.

Nor do we achieve our salvation by "claiming Jesus as my personal Savior," as many Christian fundamentalists would have it. Jesus' saving work was for the entire human race, beginning with Adam and Eve and continuing till the last human being is created. It is not something we can bring about on our own by choosing Jesus because, if it were, then many good and holy people who lived before God became human and served Him in an extraordinary manner would not have been saved. In reality, even Abraham, Isaac, Jacob, Moses, Joshua, David and all the faithful people of the Old Testament needed a Savior to come and bring about their salvation.

As we have seen previously, this is what we celebrate every time we offer the Holy Sacrifice of the Mass. It is the renewal in a sacramental form of the events of the first Holy Thursday, Good Friday, Easter Sunday and Ascension Thursday. Moreover, it is not enough to rejoice in our salvation; we must fulfill all the commands of love that Jesus has given us so as to enter into His saving work. We must claim it as our own and we do that by living according to His will. To initiate that in our lives, God gives us the Sacrament of Baptism.

Baptism is that sacrament which initiates us into the life of God Himself. It is the gift whereby we are the beneficiaries of the indwelling of the Holy Trinity. This indwelling is accomplished by the removal of Original Sin and its replacement by the gift of sanctifying grace, which we have discussed in previous pages. Recall our statement that to be in the "state of grace" is not just to be free of any serious sin but to be alive in God through the power of His grace which gives us a sharing in the life of God Himself. St. John, in his First Letter, says, "in this way the love of God was revealed to us: God sent His only-begotten Son into the world so that *we might have life through Him*." (4:8) No wonder St. Paul could exclaim, "I live, no it is not me any longer, but Christ Jesus who lives in me. I continue to live my natural life but with a deep abiding faith in Jesus who died for me." (Gal 2:20)

So the rite of Baptism is more than a rite of initiation such as would make us a member of a society or organization. It is rather an infusion of grace into our souls which brings about a radical transformation in us, a change that can be expressed as now having God living in and through us, or as St. Augustine put it, "God became man so man could become God!" Indeed, we call this rite a "Christening" primarily because, through it, we are united to Christ in such manner that we are to become Christ to one another. This is accomplished to the degree that we allow His life to energize ours and live so that others may see Him working in and through us. Therefore, living that Christian life is not just a matter of being obedient to the laws of Jesus and His Church but in owning them, letting them be the guiding force in every decision we make—and we make dozens of decisions every day. That is what the sacramental grace of Baptism is all about.

Jesus expressed this reality in a beautiful image given to His Apostles at the Last Supper. There, in the midst of His marvelous discourse, He declared, "I am the vine, you are the branches. As long as I live in you and you live in me, you will bear much fruit, but *apart from me you can do nothing."* (John 15:5) The source of all that is good is God Himself. Just as the life giving fluid or sap that flows unchanged through the vine into the branches to give them life, so also the very same life that flows through the Vine (Jesus) flows unchanged into the branches (the baptized) and that life is called "grace." The word means "gift" because it is freely given by God to all who choose to receive it.

In that way, the Lord makes Himself visible in this world. So in a very real sense, Baptism is our initiation into the very life of God so that the works He performed during His time on earth may be continued in our time. For that reason, this union of all those who are thereby alive in Christ can be called "the Mystical Body of Christ" or, as it is more frequently named, the Catholic Church.

The water used is the perfect symbol of washing away sin and pouring into the person's soul the life of God Himself. It has been said that we can live without food for 30 days but we cannot live without water for more than 48 hours. Water, then, is a vital sign of life while also being a sign of cleansing and renewal. No wonder Jesus chose it as the sign through which He would erase the effects of the sin of our first parents ("Original Sin") and enliven the soul with His own divine life. This is why we speak of Baptism as providing a new birth, a whole new way of life. To be "born again of water and the Holy Spirit" means precisely that, so when someone speaks of being a "born again Christian," what they are really saying is that they have come to a human understanding of precisely what took place at their Baptism by God's initiative, not theirs.

It is in this act of giving divine life (grace) to the baptized person that we find the reason for the priest being called "Father" since it is he whom the Lord uses to give His life to the newly reborn. Just as the human father plants his seed into a woman and thereby enables her to conceive and nourish their child, so it is that the priest as "father" implants the seed of God's divine life into the soul of the baptized which is then nourished by the many other signs and graces which holy Mother Church provides for her children. Here is one more example of his participating in the mystery of God's saving work, namely by being the instrument through which that indwelling is accomplished. But, as it always seems to be with God, there is still more!

Following the pouring of the water in Baptism, the priest then anoints the head of the person with a special ointment called "chrism." This is a special oil which can be blessed only by a bishop, usually at the special Mass of the Chrism celebrated during the early days of Holy Week and it is used for the three sacraments which can be received only once: Baptism, Confirmation and Holy Orders (Priesthood). The newly baptized person is anointed on the forehead as the minister of Baptism says, "I

anoint you priest, prophet and king." This special anointing
indicates three roles to be played by the newly baptized and,
ultimately, by the priest.

The first is that of **Priest**. This is fulfilled whenever the
person actively participates in the Sacrifice of the Mass. Through
Baptism, the person becomes an official member of the worship-
ing community. We are told in the prayer called the Morning
Offering that we offer our day "in union with the Holy Sacrifice
of the Mass throughout the world" to indicate the universality
of this act of worship.

Recall that the Mass is the sacramental re-presentation of
the Passion, Death, Resurrection and Ascension of Jesus and
in that way He continues to perform that saving work for the
entire human race. So the laity are to celebrate the Mass with
full, conscious and active participation because they share in
what our most recent popes have called "the priesthood of the
laity." By this anointing, then, the lay person is joined in a special
bond with every priest with whom they will celebrate the Mass
during their lives. Should that person go on to respond to God's
call to serve Him in the ministerial priesthood, then he will be
anointed once more with chrism so as to be energized to fulfill
that special priestly role within the life of the Church.

The second effect of the anointing with chrism is to declare
the newly baptized person a **Prophet**. As we have seen, the word
"prophet" comes from Greek and means "one who speaks for
another." Thus, the Old Testament prophets spoke on behalf of
God and proclaimed His message to His chosen people. If, in
doing so, they also foretold the future, most likely they were not
aware that they were doing so. That aspect of their proclaiming
on behalf of God was an added effect, but their primary role was
to speak for God in their time. Through this baptismal anointing,

then, the newly baptized person is empowered to speak for God in word, in action or in both in our time.

This is our role, then, as Catholics, namely to be Christ to one another. As one of our contemporary liturgical songs has it, "We are called, we are chosen, we are Christ for one another." In this connection we can recall the wondrous words of the great St. Francis of Assisi when he encouraged his followers to "preach the gospel on every occasion; if necessary, use words!" Those baptized persons who are later called to sacramental priesthood are, by that fact, called to preach the Word of God *officially*, proclaiming for God's People how they are to live the gospel values taught by Jesus and to practice what they preach. But the role of the priest as prophet was initially conferred upon him at his Baptism, as it is on all the baptized. It is through his ordination that he is raised to the level of being an official prophet of God, a preacher and teacher of God's people. That is why one of his principal duties is to preach the gospel, as St. Paul puts it, "in season and out of season, whether convenient or inconvenient." More than preach it, he is to connect it to the lives of his people, showing how they can apply it to their daily lives.

The third and final result of the anointing with chrism at Baptism is to be called **King**. This has two effects. The first is that the baptized person is now a member of the Kingdom of God with the promise of life in the eternal kingdom of heaven if he or she lives a faith-filled life. It is that goal which is to guide our every thought, word and deed.

The second effect is that the person is now capable of ruling over his or her life, not that they are in control of what happens throughout their life but that they are now truly empowered by God to make the right decisions so as to live in accord with the Lord's teachings. As we have seen, this is the purpose of the graces received in this sacrament. This applies in a unique way to the baptized person who is called to priesthood because it is then his role to lead the People of God to the Kingdom, showing them in word and deed how to live lives of faith and celebrating the Mass and sacraments in such fashion as to inspire and energize them to do so.

All of these signs are bestowed by the priest, the spiritual father of the child, and together with placing the white gown on the child (a sign of its new life in God) and giving the small candle to the godparent (lit from the Paschal Candle, the sign of the Risen Jesus in whose life the child now shares), he presents the child to the community as its newest member.

Naturally, all that has been said about the baptism of a child applies equally to any adult who is baptized and perhaps, in one sense, with even greater effect on the adult since he or she has consciously journeyed through the RCIA process of their own free will and therefore should have a greater understanding of all that is happening. Understanding it immediately or not, the ultimate reality is that the baptized person is now alive with God's life, that the Triune God, Father, Son and Holy Spirit now dwells within the soul of that person, and the priest has started the newly baptized on a journey that it is hoped will profoundly affect every aspect of their life. What an awesome privilege this is for the priest, to bring this person to a whole new level of being, a supernatural level of living in union with the Lord. It is truly a rebirth! No wonder the minister of this fundamental sacrament rejoices in the title, "Father"! He is the life-giving instrument chosen by God to bring each person he baptizes into the mystery of sharing in God's own life. From time to time he needs to reflect on this divine reality and see in each person he baptizes that new life springing into action through the various sacramental signs he is privileged to celebrate. He is truly a man of mystery!

The Sacrament of Penance

I was sitting in the Room of Reconciliation one Saturday afternoon waiting for penitents to come to Confession when in walked a woman in her mid-thirties. She appeared quite apprehensive and deservedly so, since she had never made a face-to-face Confession before. The room did offer the option of kneeling behind a screen but she chose not to use it. More to the point, she had not been to Confession for over ten years. She started nervously, struggling to recall the formulas often used to begin a Confession which her grammar school teachers had taught her, so I guided her through them. Once we had determined approximately how long it had been since her last Confession, she started to tell her sins; they were plentiful, varied and quite serious. She kept her eyes closed throughout.

When she finished, she looked up tentatively to see my reaction. I gently asked her a few simple questions to clarify the circumstances of one or two of her sins, made some suggestions as to how she could get back on track with her sacramental and spiritual life, and then said, "For your penance, I want you to go up to the front of the church, kneel before the tabernacle where our Eucharistic Lord is, and thank Him for two things: first, for the grace He gave you to come to Confession, because He is the one who inspired you to come here, and then to thank Him for this wonderful sacrament through which ten years of some pretty heavy sinning have been forgiven." "That's all?" "Yes, that's all, because you have already done enough penance getting yourself in here and telling me your sins. Besides, a prayer of thanksgiving to God said from your heart will mean more than a dozen Our Fathers and Hail Marys. Now, please say the Act of Contrition." Pretty sure that she would not remember it, I gave her a prayer card, she started to read the prayer and then, giving way to deep sobs, her tears began to flow. Rarely had I seen such deep sorrow mixed with relief. When she finished the Act of Contrition and I prayed the words of absolution over her, I dismissed her saying, "Give thanks to the Lord for He is good, His mercy endures forever. Now go in His peace."

Then she did something I will never forget. She stood up, her face still covered with tears, and said, "Father, can I ask you to do one more thing?" Wondering what that request meant, I said, "Okay." "Will you please stand up?" Tentatively, I did stand and she came forward and embraced me with a hug I will never forget. The power of God's merciful forgiveness was so evident in that woman that she felt compelled to express her gratitude to God through me in the most human of ways. She spoke a most heartfelt "Thank you, Father," and headed toward the front of the church to pray her prayer of thanksgiving. Through God's call, I had been the channel of His mercy.

Nothing that Jesus did was done without a plan. Even the most apparently spontaneous action, be it a miraculous healing or raising someone from death, was performed to fill in another part of the plan of salvation which the Father sent His Son to complete. So it was with the institution of the sacrament of Penance.

It was the first Easter Sunday night. Jesus had just completed His supreme act of redemption by dying on the Cross and rising again. Nonetheless, there was a deep fear in the hearts of the Apostles (his first priests) that those who had put their Lord and Master to death now would be looking for them, possibly to bring the same condemnation and punishment on those who had been His companions. So they locked themselves into the Upper Room where they had spent their last hours with Him before His Passion and Death and waited to see what would happen. Yes, some were saying that He had risen from the dead and had appeared to both Peter and Mary Magdalene but how could that be? They knew for sure that He had died. Indeed, one of them, the young John, was right there with Mary and the other women when the soldier thrust his spear into Jesus' side to be sure that He was dead. Moreover, with the help of Nicodemus and Joseph of Arimathea, they had placed His body in the tomb and sealed it. How, then, could it be that Jesus had appeared, now alive again, to Peter and Mary Magdalene? The Apostles knew that Jesus had brought back to life at least three other people but could He actually raise Himself from the dead?

Then it happened. Even though the doors were locked, Jesus appeared right in their midst. One can only imagine the mixture of amazement, wonder, fear and guilt that must have seized their hearts. If this really was Jesus, would He berate them, punish them, remind them of their cowardly actions, upbraid them for their lack of faith and gratitude? They trembled in fear and astonishment and waited to hear what He would say. Then He spoke those words which the angels had spoken at His birth and which were destined to become a source of courage and strength and peace to all believers down to the present day. "Peace be with you. Do not be afraid. It is I!" He was alive! He was with them! He loved them and forgave them! In their astonishment, they must have breathed a collective sigh of relief.

Then, even more significantly, we are told that He "breathed on them." The word used to describe that action is

used only one other time in the whole Bible. It is at the creation
of man and woman in Genesis. There we are told, *"The Lord God
formed man out of the clay of the ground and blew into his nostrils
the breath of life, and so man became a living being."* It was a truly
radical action that transformed the lifeless clay into the first
human being, a being, we are told, made in the very image and
likeness of God. Now the Apostles heard that verb used again
and it would radically change each of them on whom the Lord
breathed that first Easter night.

That breathing action was accompanied by the words,
*"Receive the Holy Spirit. Whose sins you forgive, they are forgiven;
whose sins you do not forgive, they are not forgiven."* Recall again
that the principal purpose of His Passion and Death, Resurrection and Ascension was to forgive the sins of the whole human
race. Now Jesus was giving to the Apostles the power to do just
that, to transmit in His name His universal forgiveness to each
individual who would seek it from them and their successors.

At one time during His ministry, a paralyzed young man
had been brought to Jesus to be cured. Instead, He started by
saying that the young man's sins were forgiven. Some of the
leaders challenged His words, indicating that only God could
forgive sins... and for once, they were right! Then, to show that
He really did have the power to forgive sins—and thereby equate
Himself with God—He said, "Arise and take your stretcher and
go home." And the young man did exactly that. However this
action and these words spoken in the Upper Room on that first
Easter Sunday evening were much more. Now Jesus was passing on that divine power so that these awe-struck men whom
He loved so much could do the very same thing He did: forgive
sins! Now they would be truly acting in the image and likeness
of God. They and their successors would become the instruments

by which He would forgive the sins of anyone who sought His forgiveness. Surely, this is one of the truly awesome powers of the Catholic priest.

What exactly is the priest's role in Confession? First of all, to forgive sins; therefore, he must know those sins in order to forgive them. This is the part of Confession that most people find difficult, yet the priest is not sitting in judgment though sometimes he must make a judgment about the degree of seriousness of the sins. That is why he will sometimes ask questions but no more questions than are necessary to make that judgment. Then he can offer some suggestions as to how those sins can be avoided in the future. He may suggest better sacramental celebrations (especially at Mass), regular prayer, some reading from the Scriptures, spiritual reading or some specific practice that will strengthen the person's resolve to resist their specific temptations.

I recall at least two instances when the suggested practice was truly a sacramental inspiration by the Holy Spirit for I would not have thought of these things on my own.

In the first instance, a mother confessed with great sincerity that she was tired of arguing with her young son who seemed constantly stubborn about doing what she asked of him. In an effort to help, I passed on the thought that at a time when she was not angry with him, she should talk to him about the situation, asking him to explain why he was so stubborn. She said she would and, to my surprise, she returned the next week, not to go to Confession but to tell me that what I had suggested had worked. She related that when she asked him why he was so stubborn, his response was that it was because she never asked him to do something, instead she always told him, even ordered him, to do it and that he would do whatever she wished if only she would just ask. She did and he did.

The second instance resulted from a woman asking me for advice to deal with someone she knew well who had spoken to her in a very crude and mean-spirited way and she was having a hard time forgiving her. I suggested that when she left the Confessional she should say two Acts of Contrition, one for herself and one for the other person, asking God to give her the grace to forgive. As in the previous case, that woman also came back the next week to say that my suggestion had worked. My suggestions? Not really. It was the Holy Spirit guiding me, as He seeks to guide all His priests when celebrating this wondrous sacrament of God's mercy.

In addition, call to mind a previous reflection in which we spoke about the need we have to *become* the sacrament, not just to receive it. Here was that grace working in both these cases and leading the first woman to ask why both she and her son were angry, and the second woman to forgive as she had been forgiven. Under the guidance of the priest as he responded to the graces of the Holy Spirit, both these women had clearly become the sacrament, signs of God's forgiveness.

As for the priest's role of assigning a penance to the penitent, while there are some priests who suggest saying prayers such as the Our Father, Hail Mary, the *Memorare*, etc., the penance could also be some specific action that will counteract the most frequently committed sin. In other words, a penance, instead of measuring the seriousness of the sins by the number of prayers to be said, could well be something constructive. So a wife who has fought with her husband might be asked to prepare his favorite meal or a husband to take his wife out for dinner. A child who confesses disobedience might be told to try to do everything his or her parents ask for the next week and to do so without complaining or asking why. (I had one mother, to whose child I had given that penance, request that "the next time, please make it two weeks. It was great!") These and similar actions are truly remedial and have the effect of positing a good action to make retribution for the bad one.

While a number of Catholics considered Confession a difficult task, perhaps even an ordeal, what they need to understand is that celebrating the Rite of Reconciliation is actually a celebration of God's Mercy. It is the fruit of the work of salvation Jesus came to accomplish and the fulfillment by the priest of the commission given to the Apostles on the night of His Resurrection. The principal reason for the Son of God becoming human, then dying, rising and ascending, was to indicate the unconditional love of the Father for us and His constant willingness to forgive us our sins once we admit them. It was through His saving work that Jesus brought this forgiveness into the world and then, through His passing on His power to forgive sins to His priests, that He made that forgiveness available to each individual who seeks it.

What a glorious gift it is to each priest that the Lord calls into His service that He bestows on him the truly divine power to forgive all those who come to Confession seeking forgiveness. Nor is that wondrous work restricted to the confessional. I personally have heard many a Confession in the hospital, at the scene of an accident, standing at a gas station, sitting in any space available, and it was always in response to the requests of the penitent who was taking advantage of the convenience of having a priest at the scene and willing to activate his power to forgive in God's name. Just as Jesus did, the priest has the high privilege of offering God's forgiveness to all who seek it and to send them away having been the recipient of the Father's Divine Mercy.

From time to time, people ask what it's like to hear Confessions. I tell them that it can be rewarding and gratifying, or tedious to the point of being boring! Rewarding because I am at that moment a channel of God's mercy and forgiveness; gratifying because of the change that a good Confession and spiritual direction can bring about in the one confessing; tedious (especially when hearing the Confessions of little children) because they're not quite prepared and they sometimes don't know just what is a sin and what isn't. Hearing Confessions is a truly awesome experience because, over a period of years, the priest's growing awareness of how unworthy he is—for he, too is a sinner—and that God nevertheless continues to use him to dispense His merciful forgiveness, provides an increasing knowledge and understanding of the reality of God's calling him to serve His people in a way of which he is totally undeserving. He is truly a wounded healer.

One last thought and it probably will answer the next question that might be asked: Do priests go to Confession, too? The answer is, of course they do! We, too, are sinners, perhaps more aware of our own frailties and faults than the average lay person precisely because we are called to a higher standard. Too often the sins we hear are the very ones we commit, so we appreciate very much this extraordinary gift of not only forgiving the sins of others but having our own sins forgiven. There are many priests who, before they begin hearing Confessions, make a fervent Act of Contrition themselves to ask God's forgiveness for their own sins, to thank Him for the power to absolve others of their sins, and to ask for wisdom and inspiration in guiding those who come to them seeking forgiveness and direction. The Sacrament of Penance and the Rite of Reconciliation are for all sinners, and that includes priests, for "to whom much is given, much will be expected."

The Sacrament of the Anointing of the Sick

There was a town employee, who was middle aged, somewhat overweight, a lukewarm Catholic who was irregular in his attendance at Sunday Mass. His wife was younger than he, the stay-at-home mother of their three children, a devout Catholic who participated in a number of parish activities. She came to me one Sunday after Mass to tell me of her concern for her husband. He had just gone for his annual physical exam and was told that his right carotid artery was 90% blocked and his left carotid artery was 70% blocked, making him a prime candidate for a stroke. He was scheduled to go to the hospital on Tuesday for an angioplasty or, if that didn't work, for heart by-pass surgery. I asked what he was going to be doing on Monday and she said he was going to work but would be free after four o'clock. I urged her to bring him to the rectory after work so I could administer the Sacrament of the Anointing of the Sick and she agreed wholeheartedly.

They arrived the next day as planned and I explained to him that the sacrament was not to prepare him for death (as someone his age might think since he had grown up knowing the sacrament as "Extreme Unction" or "the last anointing") and that it would include going to Confession and receiving Holy Communion. He agreed to receive the sacraments and so we began. Following his Confession, I anointed him on the forehead and hands saying the prescribed beautiful prayers. When I finished he said, "Wow! That's powerful!" I agreed and went on to complete the sacraments by giving him Holy Communion. When we were finished, I told them I would remember him at Mass the next day and sent the two of them on their way.

The next day I got a call from his wife telling me that when he went to the hospital the next morning, the pre-operation X-rays showed that both carotid arteries were 100% clean so there was no need for any treatment at all! That's how powerful the Sacrament of the Anointing of the Sick can be and this story is not the only incident of an instant cure in which I have been privileged to share through my priestly ministry.

At the same time that this healing took place, I was also ministering to a young mother who had a very serious cancer. Because she could not bear children, she and her husband had adopted two boys who were then age six and four. The tumor in her stomach was enormous and she had tried every possible cure, including trips to Canada to visit a doctor who specialized in her form of cancer. Nothing had helped.

When she called me to visit them, it was obvious that she was in need of the Anointing of the Sick. She and her husband were people of great faith and were bringing their sons up in the Catholic Faith as best they could. Within the next several weeks I visited her with Communion and anointed her twice. None of this brought about the desired results. While her faith remained strong, she grew weaker and weaker until she finally passed away. The whole neighborhood was affected by her loss because she had fought so valiantly and accepted her death with such peace. We even planted a tree in her memory in their housing development, a ceremony that was attended by all her neighbors, regardless of their religious affiliation.

Why tell these two stories? Perhaps because ever since they happened I have wondered about God's selectivity in granting healing. The man who rarely went to church had been completely healed; the young mother, who was so filled with faith, was not. Perhaps he needed more time to prepare to meet his Lord, but once more I was dealing with the inscrutable wisdom of God. Once more I grew in my understanding that it is *He* who acts through the sacraments and that the priest is only His instrument.

Of course, such a complete healing as the one cited in the first story is not frequent. The vast majority of those who receive this sacrament experience one of three effects: (1) they get well and resume their previous activities, (2) they recover only partially, or (3) they die. In the first instance, the medical procedures bring about their desired effect and the person resumes their normal activities. In the second instance, the person continues in their state of illness but does so with an inner peace that produces a sense of holy acceptance of their state. In the third instance, the person passes on to eternal life but does so in a peaceful state of mind, heart and soul with the realization that we are all going to die and it is better to do so being in the state of grace and prepared to meet the Lord. Whatever the result, the sacrament brings an inner peace that only God can give, one that brings the person to understand that sickness and suffering are a part of our lives and can be a time of great growth in holiness.

In the sixth chapter of Mark's Gospel, we are told that, following the instructions of Jesus to the Apostles about how they were to go out to bring the Good News of His coming to the people, "the Twelve drove out many demons and they anointed with oil many who were sick and cured them." This healing ministry commissioned by Jesus was one more way in which the Apostles and their successors were called to share in one of the most frequent events in the earthly ministry of Jesus, the healing of the sick.

Prior to the Second Vatican Council, the Anointing of the Sick was given only to those in serious danger of death and, in some instances, even after death since it is not known at what time the soul of the deceased actually left the body. This approach resulted in many people not receiving the "the last sacraments" at all since it was thought that the sick person would be frightened when the priest was called. Today, thank God, the approach is much more positive and the Anointing of the Sick is seen as a benefit to all who receive it. Many request it before going through surgery (no surgery is guaranteed 100% "safe") and it can be given periodically even to those who "are suffering the effects of advancing years," as one priest friend of mine expresses it. Indeed, when some elderly person passes away suddenly, it can be a great comfort to the family to know that the person had recently been anointed.

For the priest, the administration of this sacrament is one more wonderful way in which he is called to participate in the healing ministry of Jesus. The request for the anointing may come following weekday Mass from a daily communicant who is going in for surgery, from the spouse, son or daughter of an elderly and frail person who is growing weaker each day, from an emergency call in the middle of the night by a relative of someone who has been rushed to the hospital, or from a con-scientious administrator of a home for the aged who requests a periodic communal anointing service for the Catholics who reside there. Whatever the circumstances, the priest who carries out the anointing also benefits by receiving a sense of peaceful satisfaction at having brought at least inner healing to, and allay-ing a sense of fear from, those whom he has anointed. It is one more sign of the unconditional and eternal love of God for His people and how privileged is the priest who shares in bringing that very special sign of God's love to those who need it.

The Sacrament of Marriage

The bride sat across from me in the rectory office, her fiancé at her side. They had come to make final preparations for their wedding and were eager to share their choices of Scripture readings and songs that would be used in their ceremony. They handed me the list of readings, and I noticed they selected the most frequently requested passages: Genesis 1 (the creation of man and woman), Psalm 33 ("The earth is full of the goodness of the Lord"), 1 Corinthians 13 ("Love is patient, love is kind," etc.), and John 15 ("Love one another as I have loved you"). Just to test the waters, I asked, "Have you considered Ephesians 5 in which St. Paul gives us our theology of marriage?" The bride-to-be responded, "Isn't that the one where Paul says that wives should be submissive to their husbands in everything?" "Yes, it is," I answered, but before I could go any further, she said, "Then I definitely don't want that read at my wedding," which was not the first time I had heard that declarative statement. While I did not push the issue, I thought to myself, "How sad that readers, especially those who are preparing to enter into a marriage covenant, stop as soon as those words are read and don't bother to read the whole passage."

Why am I including a section on marriage when discussing the life of a priest? Primarily because it is the priest's role to convey to all his parishioners, but especially to those preparing for marriage, just what marriage is really all about. That passage from St. Paul's Letter to the Ephesians is essential to our understanding of the sacredness of the marriage covenant and the celebrant of the wedding should address it whether or not that particular passage will be used. So let's take a brief look at his message.

Paul is speaking of marriage and is comparing it to the union of Christ and His Church. He states, "As the Church submits to Christ, so wives should submit to their husbands in everything." Taken at face value (while putting aside for a moment the structure of marriage at Paul's time), small wonder that today's brides so quickly cast that passage aside. But what is Paul actually saying? Going back to the root of the word translated as "submit" we find that it means that wives should put their husbands first, before themselves and before their children, and isn't that what marital love is all about? This thought is further clarified in the next sentence (which usually is not even considered after the first statement is read!), when Paul declares, "Husbands, love your wives as Christ loves the Church; He gave Himself up for her!"

Even from the point of good literature, there is an interesting and challenging balance here. In other words, wives and husbands must always put their spouse first, and if this is happening consistently, then the peaceful and sacrificial love that should be the hallmark of every marriage stands a good chance of being present to enable the couple to deal with whatever difficulties arise—and they will arise—and not only preserve but strengthen their marriage. Moreover, in this particular passage, Paul goes into greater detail about how the husband must look upon his wife as Christ looks on the Church. "He who loves his wife loves himself. Observe that no one ever hates his own flesh; no, he nourishes it and takes care of it just as Christ cares for His bride, the Church, for we are members of His body." So Paul is stressing that the union of the bride and groom should be so complete that they become one, just as the human and divine natures became one in Christ.

That last statement brings us to the heart of the matter: The couple is with the priest to prepare for their *marriage*, not just for a wedding. We have noted above that all the sacraments of the Church are given so that, responding to the special graces of each sacrament we receive, we are formed more and more into the image of God and by becoming the sacrament or sign, we continue to give witness to His continuing ministry to the world. But what is it about Christ and His ministry that is continued in the Sacrament of Marriage?

Actually, it is the most fundamental thing we can say about Jesus, namely, that He is God who became man. At a specific moment in time, He joined to His eternally existing divine nature a created human nature taken from the womb of the Virgin Mary in such manner that those two natures can never be separated. The Son of God can never stop being the Son of Mary and vice versa. And why did He do this? The answer is found in John 3:16: "God so loved the world that He gave His only begotten Son so that all who believe in Him may have eternal life." God's love for us humans was the sole motivating principle that led to His Incarnation and our salvation. Therefore, just as He left us the other six signs (sacraments) of His ministry when He left this earth to return to the Father, so He left this sign of precisely who He is and why He came. Unlike the other sacraments, He did not use inanimate objects to be the signs, namely, bread, wine, oil, water and words. No, in this instance He reached back to the crowning work of His creation, man and woman who had been made in His own image and likeness for the propagation of the human race. He blessed that union so that, from that time on, the couple would receive the special sacramental graces needed to live in such depth of love and peace with and for each other that they would, in an admittedly frail and human way, become a sign of His love for all of us.

It is significant that Marriage is the only sacrament that is not administered by the priest. The man and woman administer it to each other by the public statement of their marriage vows. The role of the priest is to witness the Christian marriage and give it ecclesiastical validity. However, I would suggest that the more important role of the parish priest is to prepare the couple for their marriage (again, not just for their wedding) by stressing the sacrificial nature of their union so that they may properly and fruitfully prepare for and understand the very special covenant into which they are entering. Nor is the word "covenant" casually used here.

A sacramental marriage is not a contract because a contract lays down certain conditions and agreements that, should they be violated by either or both parties, would invalidate the contract. Instead, a covenant is a union between two people which pledges them to a total commitment to that union no matter what befalls them. It is an image of the covenant between God and His People to whom He has proven Himself to be eternally committed, no matter how unfaithful His People prove to be. However, because these are two human beings, essentially flawed due to the lasting effects of Original Sin, who are entering the union, there can be circumstances which may, in effect, ultimately invalidate that union. Nevertheless, no couple should ever enter into a marriage covenant with the attitude that, "if it doesn't work out the way I want it, we can always break the union and get a divorce and annulment," a mentality that, sad to say, seems to be growing in parts of our society.

Therefore, while the priest, by virtue of his vow or promise of celibacy, puts aside the option of marrying and raising a family, he nonetheless has a serious responsibility to see that every couple he joins in marriage enters into that union with as clear an understanding as is possible of how they are to live out their special sacrament. In this endeavor he will probably call upon some of the married couples within his parish to assist him in counseling those who are engaged. Such couples will thereby become their sacrament by the example of their own married lives but also go a step further through sharing with and instructing couples preparing for marriage. During this process those planning to be married can have clearly explained to them by the priest and his co-workers the Church's teaching on the unity and sanctity of marriage, along with her teaching on birth control and the benefits of natural family planning. They can also witness to the importance of a solid spiritual life based on faithful celebration of Mass and the sacraments, as well as instructing them on other more mundane issues such as handling finances, rearing children and dealing with in-laws.

One of the great joys that comes into a parish priest's life comes with seeing how very many successful marital unions there are in our Church and what wonderful examples such couples give of living out their commitment, thus becoming, through their sacrificial love for each other (and for their children, should God grant them children), signs of God's love for His people.

Finally, when it comes time for the wedding, the rehearsal and actual celebration, it is the priest's role to remind the couple of the seriousness of the covenant into which they are about to enter. Far too often have I seen an enormous amount of time spent in preparing for every possible aspect of the accidentals of the ceremony and the reception, rather than giving far more serious consideration to the many aspects of the union into which they are about to enter.

As one example, during our talk in preparation for her

wedding, one bride asked if the groom could first walk down the aisle with his parents to be followed by her and her parents. I thought it would be a wonderful idea. However, when we started to practice that at the rehearsal, the bride suddenly declared, "We can't do that!" I asked why not and she responded, "Because he will see me in my gown!" To which I queried facetiously, "And if he does, do you die?" "No," she answered, "but it's bad luck!" I then offered the observation that here we were, preparing to celebrate a sacrament of the Church and she was speaking about a superstition, only to have the bride's mother glare at me and state, "We're speaking about tradition!" (Guess who won that one!)

In this context, it has long been my dream—hardly ever fulfilled—that such things would happen to show that it is not just her "big day" but his, too, and even more, that the parents of the bride and groom not sit on "her" side and "his" side but would sit on the same side, even in the same bench to witness that these two families were being joined together by their children.

Now let me add one more consideration of the priest's role in this Sacrament of Marriage, namely, the example he can give about fidelity to a person's sacramental union with God. I recall a young man coming into the rectory one day asking for some advice. "I have been married for seven years, Father, and while the first years were good, I'm just not happy any longer. What should I do?" I responded by saying, "First of all, who told you that you were going to be happy all the time?" I paused till I thought that idea had registered and then went on: "You need to understand that your marriage is not about your happiness, it's about your wife's happiness, and her marriage is about your happiness. So I suggest that you go home and think hard about what you can do for her to restore that love you claim you once had and begin to think about what you can do to make her happy. Perhaps then she will reciprocate and you will re-awaken the happiness you want to have. But remember, no one is happy all the time. Do you think I'm happy when the alarm goes off at 6:00 AM and I feel rotten but I have to get up and go and celebrate Mass because there are parishioners waiting for me? Why do I do it? Because I entered into a covenant with God years ago to serve His people. He has kept His end of the agreement so I have to do whatever I can to keep mine. Please take the same approach to your marriage and don't forget to call on those special graces that come with your sacrament just as I call on the graces of mine." That young man left at least thinking about what I had told him but I never found out if it worked. Nonetheless, the lesson I was trying to teach was that both Marriage and Priesthood are about commitment, a commitment that clearly involves God.

On the day of his ordination, the priest promises to diligently strive to be as fitting an instrument for God as he can be. He is called to be "another Christ" and so he is to work each day at doing the Father's will just as Jesus did. The promise or vow of celibacy emphasizes that union but it is also in his celebration of all the sacraments and the other phases of his spiritual ministry that he reveals the depth of his love for Him who has called him into this divine union. After all, the powers he exercises are God's own powers. The message he proclaims is God's own message. The people he ministers to are God's own people, baptized or not. The sacrifice he offers is God's own sacrifice. Truly, he is a man of mystery, the mystery of being a sign of God's love for His People.

In the last decade of my time as pastor I was introduced

to and became a part of Teams of Our Lady. It is a program that originated in France and is now worldwide. Briefly, a Team consists of four to six sacramentally married couples who meet once a month to share a meal, share "highs and lows," continue studying a book, always a spiritual one but not necessarily dealing with marriage, and closing with intercessory prayer. Through mutual trust and deep sharing, I have learned much about married life and the couples have learned much about priestly life. The similarities and the differences are explored through real-life events and the mystery of God's love for all of us is increasingly revealed. Together we grow in our understanding of the abiding mystery of God's love for each of us.

PART TWO

The Mystery of What the Priest Does from Sunday Night to Saturday Morning

In addition to all the priestly ministries we have discussed, there are many other activities in which the parish priest gets involved and they are the subject of the second part of this book. They are the result of following a motto given to me by my pastor, mentor and confessor, the late Msgr. Edward Connors. He lived by the motto, "Be visible, available and empower the people." That saying has guided my ministry and that of many other priests whom he counseled and for whom he also set a living example. It is in fulfillment of that principle that we look now at the "mystery" of what the priest does when he is not celebrating the Mass, preaching the Word of God, or administering the sacraments. While the following chapters will not be exhaustive (though the work they describe can sometimes be exhausting!), they should convey a fairly accurate picture of those other "mysteries" that a parish priest experiences throughout his ministry.

CHAPTER 12

The Priest as
Counselor

At the end of a rather long session of counseling, the parishioner stood up to leave but first asked, "Father, do you ever charge for your counseling sessions?" Somewhat taken aback, I answered, "No, I don't, but why did you ask?" "Well, I've been to other counselors and they charge by the hour and sometimes quite a bit, so maybe you ought to at least think of taking a deduction on your income tax for the time you give over to people like me!" I laughed at his generous compliment but shook my head at the suggestion, closing the conversation with, "But that's my job and, as difficult as it sometimes is, it can be very fulfilling when the parishioner follows your advice and it works!"

Counseling can take many forms and be addressed to many different kinds of people in a whole array of situations. Any priest, who has been in active ministry even if for only a few years, can tell you story after story of the people who seek his input or advice and the circumstances they sometimes present. In time, I came to realize that they often have already decided what they will do but they want the priest to affirm their decision. Among the dozens of stories I could tell, let me share just three, keeping in mind how they reveal the role the Holy Spirit plays in the priest's counseling ministry.

I was fourteen years into my priesthood and had just been assigned to a suburban parish after spending twelve years teaching in two of our diocesan high schools. A few weeks after I arrived, I was notified by the parish secretary that a woman was in the rectory office and wished to speak to a priest. Being the priest on duty, I headed downstairs to the office, tossing up a quick prayer as I descended the stairs, "Please, Lord, help me to tell this woman what You want her to hear."

Entering the office, I encountered a kindly looking woman, very nicely dressed and probably in her mid-fifties. After introducing myself, I asked her what she wished to discuss. She began what turned out to be a rather long narrative about a quite complicated family matter and, as I listened, I grew more and more uneasy, wondering what I should say in response. She concluded by asking, "So what do you think I should do, Father?" Still trying to sort out all the ins and outs of her tale and wondering how I should respond to her query, I began to speak and, much to my surprise, what I said began to make really good sense. Indeed, as I continued, I thought to myself, "This is good stuff! When she leaves I'll write this down to have as a reference should someone else come in with a similar problem!"

When I finished speaking to her, she smiled and said, "Why, thank you, Father. That's really sound advice and I'll do my best to do what you have suggested. I greatly appreciate your time." With that, I escorted her to the door, said goodbye and headed back to the desk to write down what I had said to her. Much to my surprise, I could not recall a single word! That scared the daylights out of me but it also taught me that, in response to that brief prayer offered on the way down the stairs, it wasn't just I who had been speaking but the Holy Spirit who had spoken through me. That was a revelation I have never forgotten and one that has helped me to guide many people through the difficult times of their lives.

It all arises from the use of the gift of Wisdom that every Christian receives in Baptism and which is strengthened in the sacrament of Confirmation. It is not just the worldly wisdom that comes with age and experience and which enhances whatever guidance we may be called upon to give. It is the spiritual wisdom that leads us—if we are listening—to make the choices that God wishes us to make. Moreover, for the priest, it is the holy wisdom that, combined with the graces of his priesthood, leads him to fulfill his role as counselor to his people.

Joe and Amy were married for four years and had a two-year old son. Joe was a construction heavy equipment operator and Amy was an office manager in a firm located twenty-five miles from their home. I had officiated at their wedding, saw them at Mass each weekend and had baptized their first little boy, so I was somewhat taken aback when Joe called to say that he needed to talk to me because he and Amy were having marriage problems.

I have almost always worked on the principle of speaking to the party who contacted me, then their spouse, and finally the couple together. That way I have heard both their stories without interruption or response from the other. The third meeting would usually be more productive since I knew that they probably had shared their respective visits with me and had begun to work out some of their difficulties even before they came together to see me.

Joe had told me that Amy had accused him of being unfaithful because she borrowed his SUV to go shopping on a Saturday and had found a list of names on the floor of the cab. Some of the names were those of single or married women that he knew. He tried to explain to her that he was working in an AA program and one of the Twelve Steps called for him to make amends with those people whom he had offended while he was drinking. Amy knew that Joe was attending the AA meetings but she didn't believe his story. He also told me that they were expecting another child and he wanted Amy to quit her job and be a stay-at-home Mom. She did not want to do that.

When Amy came to see me, she brought up the incident of the list and admitted her feelings that Joe was cheating on her. In response to one of my questions, she stated that she had never suspected Joe of cheating before but she didn't buy his story about the list. It was then that I brought up my history with Alcoholics Anonymous, that wonderful program for those affected by the drinking of a family member or close friend. Because my youngest brother was an alcoholic, I had been in AA for several years and could attest to the truth of Joe's explanation. Happily, she accepted my explanation; but still upset at the friction that had entered their marriage, she turned to the subject of her job and Joe's desire that she leave it and become a full-time mother to their children, once the second child was born. I suggested that that should be the subject of my third meeting with the two of them.

The third meeting began with Amy defending her position on two grounds. First, she was a fine office manager and found a great deal of personal satisfaction in her job. Second, her first son was in a day care center so he was being well cared for and the same could be done when the second child arrived. She was always home in time to prepare dinner and did all her household chores on weekends. She also admitted that Joe helped her with those things. Joe asked that, because he made enough money to support his family, Amy should consider a part-time job closer to home so as to eliminate the forty minute commute and have more time with him and their two children. He understood her argument about job satisfaction but felt that her role of wife and mother should take precedence.

While listening attentively to both of them, I was also offering that prayer, "Lord, help me to tell them what they need to hear." Once again, He did it. For, as I sided with Joe and urged Amy to at least try to find a part-time job in town which would cut down on the time her son would be in day care and would not put the family in financial stress, she looked at me and said, "You know, Father, I've been thinking. Why should I have to ask some lady whom I hardly know and who is taking care of several other children besides my son, what kind of day my little boy had? I can find the answer to that question by sharing the day with him—and with the next child, too."

Joe and Amy left the rectory resolved to carry out the plan they had formulated. Amy found a part-time job in town but then came an added bonus. For when their second child was born (they now have three), Amy put an end to her working days and stayed at home to be a full-time Mom, and I had the satisfaction of knowing that, with the help once more of the Holy Spirit, I had played an instrumental part in not only helping to keep that marriage together but helping it grow.

Every priest who is sincerely concerned about the couples in his parish knows how challenging marriage problems can be. Sometimes what you say works and the problems are solved. Sometimes the couple comes to you when the feelings of both parties are running high and, after doing what you can, the best thing you can suggest is that they seek counseling with a professional marriage counselor. There are times when the problems are so deep seated and the couple's feelings are so strong that there is little you can do to save the situation, so they end up in divorce and your next step is to assist them in petitioning the Marriage Tribunal for an annulment of a marriage that probably should never have happened. If there are children involved it is a very difficult situation but in time, with both parties doing all they can not to involve the children in their differences, some degree of peace can be achieved.

Which brings me to another phase of marriage counseling and that is the meetings the priest has with a couple before they get married. As you may remember from a previous chapter, I was blessed to have had the opportunity to conduct Marriage Preparation sessions for several years and it taught me as much, if not more, than I feel I might have taught those couples who participated in them. The subjects covered were "Knowing Yourself and Your Partner," "The Art of Communication" (including how to fight fair!), "The Sacrament of Marriage" (about which most Catholics have limited knowledge, at best), "Sex and Sexuality," "Finances" and in the final twenty minutes, "Planning the Wedding."

Over the years I found that the most revealing—and therefore, necessary—topic was the first one on knowing yourself and your fiancée. It was somewhat startling to discover how many couples sitting before you, all of whom were engaged and planning their marriage, had spent very little time talking about themselves. One of the reasons is that they are so busy being socially active that they had taken very little time to stop, be still and really ponder who their spouse-to-be is but even more, who they are themselves! My question to them was, "How can you authentically offer the gift of yourself to another person when you don't really know what is in that gift?"

Each of us has a life story or background that we bring through life with us. This includes our parents, our siblings or lack of same, our ethnic heritage and socio-economic level, our education, our careers, our likes and dislikes, our faults and failings as well as our successes and joys, and so on. One of the roles of the priest during the process of preparing a couple for marriage is to speak to them about these things and help them discover those personal traits and feelings that may be a challenge in their ongoing relationship after marriage. For some it can be a painful process because they have spent considerable time concealing their faults or weaknesses in order to appear more attractive to their fiancée, but how unfair and even dishonest this is! So it is the role of the priest or one of the married couples who work with them, to prepare couples for marriage by walking them through this self-evaluation. In the process he might even reveal one or two of his own weaknesses or faults in order to demonstrate that we are all imperfect and will spend the rest of our lives trying to overcome those imperfections.

In the fifty years of my active ministry as a parish priest, I witnessed a steady increase in the use of drugs and alcohol in our society. Whether it is attributable to a perceived growth in the pressure under which so many people live today, the impact on young people of their celebrity idols doing drugs, the lack of traditional values in the lives of many, or the sense of failure in many who have not reached their dreamed of goal, is difficult to determine. Whatever the reason, the increase of and addiction to these artificial (and often deadly) stimulants is incontestable. Not surprisingly, then, when it is found in our parish families and is finally discovered and/or admitted, very often the first one the family runs to for help is the parish priest. Part of the training of many of our younger priests is directed toward this problem, but it is still difficult to deal with when confronted in a real life situation. What can the parish priest do? Let me offer an example.

My first encounter with an alcoholic took place on my first assignment, a rural parish in the midst of a busy resort area. I knew him through his children who were in our Teenage CYO program. They often spoke of their mother but rarely of their father. It was not until I got a call from the local police about his creating a nuisance in a local pub that I discovered why. As is the case with many of those who are afflicted with this self-destructive disease, he was a friendly, even charming guy who had polished those virtues to perfection to convince people that he was just a "social drinker" and not an alcoholic. Nonetheless, his family was disrupted and even embarrassed on many an occasion which finally led his wife and his children—both teenagers—to do an intervention by which, in effect, they said to him, "Either you go into a detox and rehabilitation center right now and get yourself sober or move out and find some other place to live." An intervention is a prime example of the proverbial "tough love" in its most painful form.

Happily, their father complied, learned to control his drinking and returned home to remain sober for the rest of his life. I recall to this day the time he stopped into the rectory to tell me about the wonderful Wedding Anniversary cruise from which he and his wife had just returned and he said rather proudly, "Father, the best part of it was that it was all done on booze money," that is, money that would otherwise have been spent on alcohol. Sadly, it was only a few years later that he passed away, his death caused primarily by the effects his drinking had on his body, but those last few years together as a family were among their very best.

Too many people still think that unless you are falling down drunk or lying in the street, you really aren't an alcoholic; you've just had "too much to drink." There are many alcoholics who can function during the week ("I never missed a day of work") but then go on binges in the evening or on the weekend, to cite just one example. In many instances, the way the parish priest gets involved results from a member of the drinker's family comes to the rectory looking for some advice as to how to deal with the problem.

Because of that first experience and the couple of priests I had met who were alcoholic, I developed an interest in the problem and began to research ideas on how to advise those who were confronting it. I encountered little of the problem during the next twelve years when I was teaching in an archdiocesan high school. The kids might have drunk on the weekends but there was little evidence of drinking on school property. However, my subsequent return to parish work brought me into contact with it again. With study, I developed a set of pretty good answers to those who were dealing with the problem, usually the family but rarely the alcoholic himself or herself. My advice was to try to talk the drinker into going to an AA meeting but, just as important if not more so, to get themselves into an AA program so they could learn to deal with their own feelings and emotions in relation to their alcoholic. Intellectually, I knew there was little they could do about the drinker, outside of an intervention, but I grew increasingly aware that they themselves needed care and the best source for that was Alcoholics Anonymous. Little did I know that some day I would have to heed my own advice.

You see, although he showed no signs of the problem while

growing up and into his early adult years, the youngest of my three brothers developed into a full-blown alcoholic in his late thirties after suffering serious reversals in his business career. By that time he was living in the Southwest so I only learned about his drinking through the calls I received from his wife. I had never experienced the problem in my immediate family so I could not imagine that one of my brothers was actually an alcoholic. (How easy it is to give advice to others but difficult to be objective and follow it yourself.) Soon the regular calls from his wife convinced me that she was right.

The story of his problem could be the subject of another book. His drinking cost him his job, wrecked his marriage and alienated his daughter, while his son, although often frustrated and confused, remained very loyal to the end. To make a very long story quite short, my brother ultimately came to live with me in the rectory of my first pastorate and there I had to confront the problem head-on. That led me to join an AA group myself and, to this day, I consider it the second greatest grace of my adult life, the first grace being, of course, my priesthood.

In the space of about a year, I had gotten him into six detox centers and four rehab centers, none of which worked because he wouldn't let them work. Finally, at one of those detox centers, the counselor said to me, "I will admit your brother only on condition that you join an Al-Anon program." By that time I was willing to do anything to put a stop to the craziness that was disturbing my life as well as my brother's. I canceled two parish appointments for the next day and went to be interviewed by the counselor. It took only a few skilled questions from him to see that I was angry, confused and resentful but I had no problems! Once the light bulb went on in my head I realized that I had some quite serious problems and Al-Anon would provide the answers. So committed was I to the program that my mother died early on a Tuesday morning and I was at my meeting that Tuesday evening. And it worked.

Not only did I finally get the courage to get my brother to leave the rectory but also to turn him down when, obviously drunk, he called me two weeks later from California asking me to send him a ticket back home. "Wherever you are, Bob, that's your home," I said and hung up the phone, placing him squarely in God's care.

To make a very long story short, it took him three years to get sober but he spent the last four years of his life in sobriety. Not only did it teach me how to deal with my feelings about my brother and his drinking and accept that I had become a world class enabler, but it also served to make me a much better priest and counselor for those who had to deal with alcoholism either in themselves or a loved one. It also taught me two great life lessons which I have preached many times: Get the word "blame" out of your vocabulary because blaming someone else for your actions is a "cop out." It amounts to saying that someone else can make you do something that's wrong without your accepting personal responsibility for your choices. We have two millennia of martyrs who testify to being able to choose even death over denying one's faith. It also taught me that I have choices and I don't have to buy into something that can be wrong or at least do me harm.

Indeed, with my brother's permission, in an occasional homily or bulletin article I made reference to his drinking problem and my role in dealing with it and, once that was known, a number of my parishioners felt free to come for advice because they felt I knew what they were going through. It also introduced many of my parishioners to the fact that priests are also human and often have to deal with the same problems that they do. We, too, are weak, frail human beings who are "wounded healers." Why, to the surprise of some, we even commit sins and go to Confession regularly! So many see and hear us only in church that they think we have no problems. What they fail to remember is that because we, too, are members of the human race, we are therefore subject to the effects of Original Sin. However, in spite of our weaknesses, the Lord who called us to be His priests provides the sacramental graces we need to carry on with His work, even while dealing with our own faults and failings. The priest who remembers this will be a more compassionate, and therefore a more successful counselor who will be very slow to judge others but eager to reach out and help in whatever manner he can. Perhaps all he can do is make a referral to the nearest AA or Al-Anon group but that in itself could very well be the opening of the door to the beginning of the recovery process for the person suffering from the disease of alcoholism, as well as all those affected by his or her addiction.

CHAPTER 13

The Priest as Consoler

The process of healing is part of the post-Vatican II Church that has received a great deal of attention. Not only is the priest seen as healer, and a wounded healer at that, but there are those among the consecrated religious and the laity who have also been given this wondrous gift. Nonetheless, it is the priest who is seen as the principal healer because of his role as minister of the sacraments, especially those of Penance, the Eucharist and the Anointing of the Sick.

We have seen in the section on the Anointing of the Sick how the priest plays the role of God's channel through which He bestows His healing grace, but there are other kinds of healing which are frequently parts of the parish priest's daily ministry to his people.

In almost every instance where there is an impending death of a parishioner, there is also a family to be cared for and guided through the process of getting prepared for the departure of their loved one and then going through all the steps that follow from the death through the wake, the Mass, the burial and the period of mourning. The priest is often called upon to be involved in all of these steps and it is often the care and concern that he shows in these special times that will be remembered many years later by those to whom he has ministered.

The whole process can begin with a call from a family member telling us that a relative is very sick and may not "make it." The priest responds to the call either by arranging a good time for a home or hospital visit or by contacting the sick person's home if the caller is not living there. That first visit can reveal a number of things. The first is how seriously ill the patient actually is. Then the priest's role is to speak to the patient about the possibility that his illness may be terminal and the need for preparing to meet the Lord. This is not an easy task but should not be shied away from. Of equal importance is encouraging the patient to join their sufferings to those of Jesus, telling them that such sacrificial suffering can bring them great grace at a time when grace is truly needed, as well as lead to the bestowal of many graces on those to whom God chooses to give them. Such thoughts can help them to see the power there is in suffering and give them a deeper understanding of what the sick person is experiencing. This preparation is then followed by the administration of the Sacraments of Anointing, Penance and Eucharist.

Jesus did not save the world by His teaching or miracles but by His Passion, Death and Resurrection, and because we are united with Him since our baptism, He gives redemptive power to all of our suffering. As we read in Romans 8, "The Spirit Himself tells us... that we are heirs of God, heirs with Christ, if only we suffer with Him so as to be glorified with Him. I consider the sufferings of the present to be as nothing compared to the glory to be revealed in us." Clearly, then, pain and suffering are a part of the human experience. The pain can be physical, psychological or emotional, but whatever form it takes, it is real.

So the role of the priest is first of all to encourage the patient to offer the pain to the Father by joining it to the sufferings of His Son and thereby participate in His redemptive work. This is what St. Paul meant when he said that we must make up what is lacking in the sufferings of Christ (Col 1:24), not that Jesus' sufferings were inadequate to save us but that we, through our union with Him, are to turn our sufferings over to the Father through Jesus and thus play our part, together with Jesus, in His saving actions. Nor should we forget the last sentence of the previously quoted passage: *"I consider the sufferings of the present to be as nothing compared to the glory to be revealed in us."*

By sharing this teaching with the family of the suffering person, the priest is also instructing them about how they can help their loved one prepare to meet God, should that be the outcome of the illness. Sometimes such an instruction is even more beneficial to the family since the sick person frequently knows how sick they are and what the possible outcome may well be. It is also quite possible that those attending the sick relative may need more reassurance than the patient does because they fear the loss of their loved one more than the patient fears death. Indeed, this fear of their loss too often keeps them from summoning the priest and the sacraments until the patient is unconscious and unable to hear the words of the sacramental ministration and thereby benefit from them. This impending loss, then, can become a very fruitful learning period for all concerned and, if properly handled, may well lead to a deepening of faith for all concerned. Nor should this be a one-time visit. The conscientious priest will follow up the initial house call or hospital visit with further visits so as to enable the patient to receive their Lord in the Eucharist and renew and reinforce his teaching on the value of suffering and the peace that only God can give in such a situation.

In the event that the illness leads to death, the priest's work now shifts to consoling the family and assisting them in the preparation for the wake, the Mass of Christian Burial and the interment. Especially if this is the first death in the family, he will guide them in their dealing with the funeral director, assuring them that the director has a regular process by which he will take the body to the funeral parlor, assist them in setting a date and times for the wake and Mass, purchasing the casket, selecting a memorial card, providing the clothes for the deceased, and all the other steps that need to be taken. The priest may also suggest that a family member connect with the parish Music Director to arrange the music selections for the Mass, and provide them with the options for the Readings so that they are truly participants in the whole process of celebrating their loved one's participation in the mystery of the Death and Resurrection of Jesus. Depending on whether the diocese permits a eulogy, the priest can provide guidelines for its contents and perhaps suggest that it be given at the wake, the burial or the consolation luncheon rather than at the Mass. In all of these matters, he becomes the source of great compassion, direction and strength to all those involved. He himself will make a genuine effort to compose a homily that reflects his knowledge of the deceased's life, even if that information is gathered only as recently as at his visits or at the wake, thus adding even more to the parish support of its people at a difficult time.

All of the above presupposes that the sick person and their family have had time to prepare for their loved one's death. As difficult as this may be, the role of the priest is often more intensely difficult when the death comes suddenly and more tragically. A sudden heart attack, an accidental death, a suicide, the death of a child, of a young single person, a young spouse or parent brings with it a whole other set of circumstances that will call upon the priest to reach into the depths of his knowledge, experience, compassion and spirituality in order to bring order and peace, consolation and strength to those involved. When handled well and in a loving manner, such pastoral care will usually bring a deeper and hitherto unknown appreciation of the priest's role by the family involved and provide for them a long lasting memory of how their priest was right there with them in a time of great need. It is at such times that the parish priest truly merits the title, "Father."

Probably the two most difficult deaths to deal with are a suicide and that of an unborn or little child. Both are devastating to the deceased's family. In the case of the suicide, the parish priest has two main goals: to assure the family that the dead person is not automatically in hell and to help them come to realize that there was probably little, if anything, they could have done to prevent it.

For centuries, the Church taught that taking one's own life led to eternal damnation, an idea that resulted in a horrible feeling within the suicide's immediate and extended family. This resulted from the conclusion that a suicide is tantamount to an act of murder, indeed, more heinous because it was the taking of one's own life. As a result of more recent studies in psychology and theology, the Church has come to realize that the act of taking one's own life flies in the face of the most fundamental force that drives us throughout our life, namely, the instinct of self-preservation. Therefore, we now understand that suicide is a highly irrational act and therefore the guilt once attached to it is considerably mitigated, removing the concept of eternal damnation in situations where the suicide is due to mental deficiency.

Indeed, the prayers given us in the Order of Christian Funerals for the Mass of one who commits suicide speak of the abiding mercy of the Lord. *"God, lover of souls, you hold dear what you have made and spare all things for they are yours. Look gently on your servant and, by the blood of the cross, forgive his/her failings. Remember the faith of those who mourn and satisfy their longing for that day when all will be made new again in Christ, our risen Lord."* And again, *"Almighty God and Father of all, you strengthen us by the mystery of the cross and with the sacrament of your Son's resurrection. Have mercy on our brother/sister. Forgive all his/her sins and grant him/her peace. May we who mourn this sudden death be comforted and consoled by your power and protection."* If possible, the priest will follow up with the family to provide ongoing assurance based on the Lord's eternal mercy and compassion.

The second very difficult case is the death of an unborn child or one who dies at a very young age. What is needed more than anything else at such a time is a great sensitivity to the feelings and emotions of the parents and other family members. I have had a number of such instances from a case of stillborn twins to the death of a 3-year-old little girl.

Among other things, the first revealed to me in a remarkable way the "brotherhood" so often spoken of among firefighters. I was called to the hospital to baptize the stillborn twins which were still in the mother's womb. Then we spoke of what plans the couple wanted to make and, after offering several options, the parents decided that they would have a regular Mass of Christian Burial. It was truly a most difficult emotional experience but the Mass was very well attended and celebrated. Then we journeyed to a large cemetery in the Bronx for the burial. It was a cold, raw and rainy day which added to the sadness, but when we arrived at the place of burial with the two tiny caskets, every member of the father's firehouse and their wives were waiting at the grave to participate in the service. It was one of the most powerful examples of compassion that I have ever witnessed.

The death of a little child also is extremely difficult to deal with but the Lord provides coinciding events to give strength to those involved. I saw this in an extraordinary way in the case of a little girl who was suffering from brain cancer and whose death was inevitable. One day, after taking her nap, she told her mother that a beautiful man had come into her room and spoke to and played with her. Naturally, the child's mother was startled and concerned but when she asked the child to describe the man, the little one pointed to the illustrated cover of a book about angels on their coffee table and said, "That's him there!" Startled but now somewhat comforted, the mother breathed a sigh of relief. A few days later the child told her that the man had come again and this time he told her that she was going to heaven very soon but that she shouldn't worry because someday her mother and father and siblings would join her there.

Soon after, the child passed over to the Lord but that angelic promise still carries those parents through the difficult times that they have faced in ensuing years. Imagine being assured by an angelic messenger that you will attain your goal of heaven, a gift unlike any other I have ever heard!

Granted, these are unusual stories, but it was my privilege as their pastor to share those events with those parents and their families and to minister to them in the best way I could. Was my participation a drain on my own personal emotions? Of course it was, but it was well worth the investment of time, energy and compassion to be able to minister to those families, along with quite a few others whom I have met in somewhat similar situations, and thereby bring the compassion of Jesus into their lives in a clear and meaningful way. Each of them provided one more way in which a parish priest grows in the realization of how privileged he is to serve God's People.

CHAPTER 14

The Priest as
Spiritual Director

G iven the enormous pressures and the hectic pace at which we live, there is a great need in our contemporary Church for people to receive spiritual direction. Such direction provides advice and suggestions as to how they can improve their prayer life, strengthen their efforts to overcome sinful ways, develop a deeper trust in God particularly in difficult times, discuss and resolve their concerns about the spiritual lives of their children, confront the spiritual aspects of dealing with an addiction and similar situations that pertain to their relationship with God and others. Nor should we think of spiritual direction as something only for those who are in religious life or ordained to the priesthood or permanent diaconate. Our spiritual life plays a direct role in how we live the rest of our lives, so it should be the concern of every person who is seeking happiness in this life and in the life to come.

To be honest, from the point of view of formal preparation, today's younger priests are probably better trained to deal with such matters. In the era in which I was ordained (the '50s), spirituality was thought to pertain primarily, if not exclusively, to priests and religious. The lay person was to simply fulfill their basic responsibilities in reference to religious practices in their lives, namely attend Mass, receive the sacraments, say their prayers and do some spiritual reading. However, one of the fruitful outcomes of the Second Vatican Council (1962-65) is an increased understanding of the important role to be played by the laity in the life of the Church. After all, they greatly outnumber priests and religious while comprising the vast membership of the Mystical Body of Christ. If—as we have seen—each one of us is called to service in God's name by the very fact of our Baptism into Christ, then much more must be done so that lay persons can function on a higher level of spirituality than previously thought.

While there are still only a relatively small number of Catholics who seek individual spiritual direction, the great majority of them being women, those who became actively involved in the liturgical and para-liturgical life of the Church also came to realize their need for guidance and support and they often inspired others to do so leading to the growth of prayer groups.

In addition, the rapid growth of prayer groups, especially those that fostered charismatic prayer, required guidance and direction if they were to be fruitful. There was a need, of course, for their approach to be orthodox, that is based on sound doctrine and not just religious feelings and emotions, and so the lot fell to those "professionals" (priests and religious) who had been involved in more advanced forms of spirituality prior to the Council. For better or worse, the parish priest soon was sought out to be the source of that direction. Truth be told, there were many who did not feel equipped to fulfill that role. Their own spiritual life might have been advanced but they often lacked the skills, training and confidence to communicate that to others, primarily because they had never been trained to do so. Moreover, the external expression of charismatic prayer style was foreign to many priests who had been trained in a more formal and structured way of praying in public or at least in small groups, so they felt awkward when asked to be a prayer leader and often backed off from doing so.

In ensuing years, two things have happened: the charismatic prayer style has become a bit more reserved, the priests have been better trained to lead such prayer and, perhaps more important, developed a comfort zone when asked to direct the individual seeking growth in his or her spiritual life. Many of us older priests have become successful in giving such direction by taking our own prayer life beyond the structured and private styles we were taught and by opening ourselves to the Spirit as He manifested Himself through members of the laity. In short, we came to understand that *all* baptized Christians are, by the very fact of their Baptism, called to develop as deep a relationship with God. Moreover, a steadily increasing number of opportunities to attend courses and lectures on the subject, coupled with a strong desire and concentrated effort to deepen one's own prayer life, has led to a number of non-ordained religious and lay persons entering the field of spiritual direction. "The Spirit blows where He will" and He is calling some Church members who are not ordained or professed religious to join their ranks. But even here, it often falls to the priest to be the instructor and guide so that together they both grow spiritually.

Granting all the above, the majority of people seeking some growth in their own relationship with God still will go to the priest for spiritual direction. While this can take place during the celebration of the Sacrament of Penance, to be truly beneficial, it needs more time than is available during parish Confessions so, for the best results, a special appointment is often sought. Indeed, one of the most satisfying aspects of a priest's ministry is to encounter such a person and become their spiritual director for as long as it is suitable for both. While such direction sometimes encroaches on what is an already crowded daily schedule, few involvements bring as great a joy to the priest as having one or more of his parishioners seek spiritual direction and then grow in their individual spiritual life.

CHAPTER 15

The Priest as Liturgist

Since leading his people in worship can be said to be the primary duty of the priest, it carries with it the mandate to provide the finest worship possible. We have already dealt with his role as another Christ possessing the authority to proclaim the Word of God and then bring about the transubstantiation of the bread and wine into the Body and Blood of Christ so He can be offered in sacrifice to the Father and then to the People of God as their Food. In that capacity, he must first prepare himself to fulfill his role. This preparation should include an attitude of genuine prayer, a study of the words of Scripture, reflection on the time and liturgical season in which he will celebrate the Mass and, from time to time, reflection on the words he is given to speak during the liturgy so that they never become merely a rote recitation.

In addition, it is the priest's role to provide a fitting worship space in which to celebrate the liturgy. Whether it be in a cathedral or in a small country church, the site must be clean, kept in good repair, well lit and heated, have a good sound system and be handicap accessible. There should be an altar, tabernacle, chairs, crucifix, chalice and ciborium, books containing the necessary prayers and directions (Sacramentary) as well as the Readings (Lectionary), candles, water, wine and cruets to hold them. In addition, there should be clean linens and vestments, plus sufficient appointments—statues, paintings, symbols, etc.—to properly designate it as a place in which reverent and fruitful worship can take place. None of these items should cost more than the parish can afford but they should be attractive, well-maintained, dignified and appropriate. If someone is hired to fulfill these tasks, they should be well-trained and held accountable for the cleanliness and orderliness of the building as well.

Since the Second Vatican Council, the laity have played an increased role in our liturgies. There are Lectors who read from the Scriptures, Extraordinary Ministers of Holy Communion, as well as Music Ministers who lead the assembly in sung worship, often with cantors, a choir and a variety of instrumentalists. All of these ministers need to have instilled in them the need to perform well without making it a performance. While he may not have time to take on the training of all these ministers, especially those involved in the music, it is the role of the parish priest to see that they are all properly trained and aware of the special position they hold in every act of parish worship in which they participate. Moreover, special services, for example those celebrated during the Triduum in Holy Week or First Communions or Confirmations, should be rehearsed so that everyone knows what they are to do before they enter the sanctuary.

The constant theme running throughout all liturgical celebrations ought to be, "We do what is called for in the Sacramentary and/or ritual and we do it as well as it can be done." Caution should be had against introducing objects or activities that are not called for in the rituals or Sacramentary. Clearly, then, the parish priest is the one primarily responsible for making all worship in his parish reverent and inspiring for himself, for the other ministers and, most of all, for his people.

Finally, the parish priest has been the traditional trainer of the altar servers. They are vital to the proper carrying out of the liturgy and should be well-trained, not only in what they are to do during the liturgical celebrations but in understanding why they do it. Today's youth are beset by so many distractions and, in many cases, are so over programmed in their extra-curricular lives that it often is difficult to get them to simply stand erect or sit still during a liturgy, to say nothing of their often distracting footwear, costume jewelry and hairdos! It is precisely to overcome this almost constant motion, which can be so distracting to the assembly, that the *why* of their presence in the sanctuary and the duties they are to perform must be thoroughly explained and reinforced from time to time. Obviously, the parish priest should be the one who delivers this message. Further, with the advent in many parishes of girl altar servers, it is important for them, too, to understand that serving at the altar is a great privilege, one to be taken on with a true sense of reverence and dignity. Finally, if the parish priest's schedule does not allow him the time needed to properly train the servers, it nevertheless remains his duty to see that these values are instilled through the person taking his place.

CHAPTER 16

The Priest as Preacher/Homilist

When I was ordained in 1956, priests gave sermons; now we give homilies. What is the difference? Before the revision of the Lectionary (the collection of readings assigned for each Mass) following the Second Vatican Council, the readings from the Scriptures at Mass were set for each Sunday. Moreover, there were only two readings each Sunday, the Epistle and the Gospel, with a Psalm in between. That meant that there were fifty-two sets of Readings, one for each weekend, and they never changed. Even the readings for such major feasts as Easter, Christmas and the last three days of Holy Week were, for the most part, always the same from year to year. This held true for the weekday Masses as well. While this may seem to have been an easier situation for the priest preparing his sermon than what is now, it presented quite a challenge to keep from repeating the same sermon on the same Sunday year after year. Sadly, some priests never met the challenge. Moreover, sermons tended to be more moralistic than instructive or Scripture based.

However, writing them also could be a spur to personal growth. I recall writing out the first sermons I gave after ordination thinking they were really pretty good. After all, I thought they reflected the fine seminary education I had received. Two years later I was transferred to a new assignment and took out those sermons to use them, thinking I had a new audience so I could put them to good use. Reviewing them, I was appalled at how weak they were, how reflective of the fact that they were my first real effort at preaching. I quickly put them into the circular file and launched out anew.

One of the great changes brought about by the Council was a much stronger emphasis on the Bible, on its study and interpretation. This led to a greater emphasis on one of the priest's principal roles, namely, to proclaim the Word of God to His people in a truly meaningful way. It called for a renewed dedication to the study of the Scriptures on the part of many priests who had been told upon ordination that they then knew everything they would ever need to know about the Church's teachings. Indeed, one of the older priests passed on a story about a young priest who was going to speak to a group of parishioners about the Scriptures. The aging pastor gave him one piece of advice: "Stay away from the Old Testament, Father; it's a mess!"

The post-Vatican II era required a whole new Lectionary. In order to introduce a greater variety of readings to the people assembled for Mass, two new arrangements were developed. The first was for Sundays and it was composed of three cycles (Years A, B, and C) which provided three times as much Scripture material for the preacher to use over a period of three years. In addition, instead of two, three readings were now assigned to each Mass, usually one from the Old Testament, one from the New Testament (the Letters, the Acts of the Apostles and Revelation) and one from the Gospels. The second arrangement was for Weekdays and it was composed of two cycles (Years I and

II). The purpose was to expose the people to much more of the Scriptures than before. The term "homily" was also introduced, as well as "homilist" for the deliverer, indicating that the priest was to dig deep into the Scripture readings and explain their contents to the people. Following the explanation of the text as well as the context in which it was written, the teaching was then to be applied to the daily life of the people so as to make the readings relevant. It was also strongly suggested that a homily be given at every Mass, not just on Sundays, which placed on the homilist a greater need for sufficient preparation and study.

Herein lies the great new challenge for the post-Vatican II parish priest. Not only is he called upon to enter more deeply into the study of the Scriptures, their cultural and historical background and deeper meaning but, in order to make them of real value to his listeners, he is urged to show how these readings can be applied to their daily lives. To assist with that challenge, a number of so-called "homily helps" have been developed by various publishers which provide an explanation of the origins, context and meanings of the text as well as some points of interest, together with a story or two that might be worked into the homily. Of course, the priest then has to take the information and ideas thus provided and fashion them into a presentation that reflects his own style and, more importantly, have meaning for the particular people to whom he was speaking so that they can be truly fed on the Word of God and take that Word and live it out in the week just beginning.

Recognizing the need for growth in his own life and that of his people, it is the responsibility of the homilist to fashion a homily to which they can relate and from which they will be inspired to work more diligently at growing in their prayer life and their daily words and actions. This presents an ongoing challenge to the homilist, one in which he is wise to seek the daily assistance of the Holy Spirit, the real author of those Scriptures. Further, as noted above, it is never enough for him to speak about the Scripture texts and explain them to those present; he must also make a practical application of their content to the lives of those who are listening. One of the wonderful by-products of this challenge is the interior spiritual growth that the priest himself experiences as he seeks to apply the Word of God to his own life as well as to the lives of his flock. In addition, there are few remarks as gratifying to the homilist as having a parishioner say, "You really gave me something to think about today, Father." That means he has done his job; he has listened to the Holy Spirit and fed his people.

CHAPTER 17

The Priest
and Youth

It almost goes without saying that when you are a young priest, you will be put in charge of whatever Youth Program the parish has in existence. The outreach to the young people of our parishes is of increasingly great importance for several reasons. Whether they attend parochial school or a public school and the Religious Education Program, their formal education in the Catholic Faith usually ends with graduation or Confirmation. It shouldn't but it usually does. It is therefore important that the parish priest do everything in his power to see that the young people do not equate their graduation or Confirmation with the end of their religious upbringing. That would be the same as stopping all academic education when one graduates from any elementary school or half-way through high school if that is when Confirmation is celebrated. So one of the primary roles of the parish priest—indeed, one mandated by the Code of Canon Law—is establishing and maintaining a strong Religious Education program.

This can take several forms. One is the continuation of religious education into the high school years. To accomplish this goal, some parishes have moved the age of receiving the sacrament of Confirmation to one of the high school years so as to retain connection with its teenagers during this critically important time of their personal formation. Whatever the chosen procedure, the courses should be structured to address those areas of faith and moral development that are so crucial to this period of personal growth. Subjects such as dating, a healthy social life, maintaining one's virginity, rules for social interaction, dealing with prejudice and bigotry, standing up for one's Faith, abortion, parent-child relationships, sibling relationships, applying the Gospel values to daily life, regular participation in Mass and the Sacrament of Penance, marriage preparation, priesthood and religious vocations, and other similar courses should be offered to all high school students.

It should be obvious that this calls for the parish priest to play an important role in the preparation and presentation of these and other suitable topics by either presenting them himself or enlisting the assistance of qualified parishioners or even non-parishioners. Since not all priests relate well to teenagers, it is imperative that he at least makes sure that the content of the presentations made by others is well-founded in Church teaching. To these presentations there should be added an occasional religious experience, perhaps a Holy Hour or a Mass for Teenagers, that is, one in which the music will be especially appealing to them and the homily focuses on matters of genuine interest to them. They should also be active participants by doing the Readings, presenting the Gifts, serving at the altar and, where possible, being part of the Music ministry for that Mass. In this way, the priest is introducing them to the proper understanding of the mysteries being celebrated, develops a closer relationship with them, and perhaps even uses the homily time to instruct them about the various parts of the Mass so they can gradually participate more intelligently and fruitfully.

If possible, the Youth Program should also include social events such as dances, bowling, skiing, bike hikes, picnics and the like. These contribute much toward the youth of different ages interacting with one another, establishing the parish as a center of their lives while they come to see the parish priest in a more relaxed setting other than in the sanctuary or in the classroom. Once again, the priest should at least be present at these events even if he cannot participate in some of them.

Finally, for the past twenty years or more, we have seen an increase in the hiring of Youth Ministers to lead these programs for teens. Resulting from the shortage of priests and the resulting decrease in the time he can give to such programs, the advent of personnel specifically trained to lead a Youth Group has made it possible to expand the outreach to our high school students. Moreover, that same person could also develop a program for the young adults in the parish, especially those who have either finished college, did not go to college, are still single and are searching for a good Catholic atmosphere in which to socialize and grow in their Faith. However, the hiring of such a person should not result in non-participation in their events by the parish priest. Not only will his presence, whenever possible, provide additional opportunities to get to know the youth involved, but it will also allow him to see how well the Youth Minister is doing their job.

The hoped for by-product of all these programs is that today's young Catholics will develop a stronger attachment to the Church and be better armed against the secular neo-paganism that surrounds them as well as the self-centeredness that today's society often produces. It is also hoped that such programs will produce more candidates for the priesthood and the religious life, a critical need for the Church in the world, today and in the future. So in all of these activities, the parish priest must play a central role, if only by encouraging the establishment of such programs and then enlisting either well-qualified volunteers or paid personnel to carry them out. Of course, this requires some of his precious time but it can be well argued that there is probably no part of his parish population that needs his priestly presence and involvement more than this particular age group. Indeed, given the state of today's culture and the diminishing number of parish priests, the future of the Church depends on such undertakings.

CHAPTER 18

The Priest and the Parish School

Although this is a difficult time for our Catholic schools, primarily because of increased tuition and operating costs as well as the absence of religious sisters and brothers from the faculty, still every step possible is being taken to preserve as many of those schools as possible. Happily, there are still many parochial schools not only still in existence but thriving. Indeed, because of shifts in population, there are new schools being built in places where none had previously existed. If there is such a school as part of his parish, what is the parish priest's role in its operation? There are several tasks he can perform.

The first is his role in the parish as the principal teacher of the Catholic Faith. In my time, I have encountered a number of pastors who never set foot inside a school classroom to instruct the students in the Faith and to assist those lay teachers who are called upon to teach it. "I leave that to the teachers," is their response. Realistically, many of our lay teachers have not had a good learning experience in the Faith and therefore cannot move beyond the textbook to share their own Faith experience with the children. Some of them are not even faithful about weekly Mass participation. The parish priest should play a major role in going into the classrooms of his school to "fill in the gaps" which the teachers cannot fill either through lack of training or failure to practice the Faith they profess.

The rapport between the priest and the students, as well as the principal and teachers, can serve well to establish a relational bond that will reinforce their desire to participate in Mass each weekend. It also allows the priest to get to know better the persons who direct the faith formation of the children, to counsel them, provide spiritual direction and instruction, and thereby play a significant role in shaping the teachers' lives as well as those of the students.

Moreover, there is a very important side effect to his visits: the children will get to know him and know that he cares about them and, who knows? Perhaps some of the young boys whom he teaches will decide that, because of his example, they would like to become a priest "just like him"! What a wonderful thing that would be, especially at this time of a growing priest shortage.

The second role of the parish priest is to be sure that the principal is actively involved in the practice of his or her Faith. Since the main purpose for establishing and maintaining a parish school is to foster the Catholic Faith, the principal cannot fully invest himself in the school's operation if he does not believe in that Faith or, if baptized into the Faith, does not live it fully. Initially, the judgment as to the principal's competence in school matters is best left to the diocesan education officials. Further, once that faithful practice of their religion and their competence in serving as principal is established, then the hiring and firing of teachers should be left to the principal, with consultation with the pastor whenever it is desired. However, if the principal's lifestyle veers from regular practice for whatever reason, the parish priest, presupposing his proximity to the situation, should exercise his leadership and deal with the problem in a discreet and productive manner.

The third consideration is the textbooks that are used in the religion classes. It is the priest's responsibility to see that they truly instruct the children in the fundamentals of our faith, that they provide real assistance to the teacher in sharing the faith with the children, that they produce in the children at least a basic understanding of the Church's fundamental teachings and offer concrete examples as to how the students should live their faith.

Of course, it will often be the role of the parish priest in the school to celebrate Mass for the school children and faculty and any parents who wish to be present. This would call for a special preparation of the homily so that it applies specifically to the lives of the children. The music should also be suitable for the children's participation while using the same melodies for the acclamations (*Glory to God; Holy, Holy; Acclamation of Faith; Great Amen* and *Lamb of God*) as are used at the parish Masses. This serves as excellent preparation for enabling the children to take an active part in the parish Mass each weekend with their families.

Throughout the year there should be some para-liturgies which are celebrations that do not include Mass but often include a Liturgy of the Word. Some examples would be on School Opening and Closing Day, a pre-Thanksgiving holiday service, Ash Wednesday observance, and Stations of the Cross during Lent. These could be led by the principal or a religious or lay staff member but the presence and participation by the priest adds a whole new dimension, perhaps through a brief homily, a special blessing or even Benediction of the Most Blessed Sacrament. These also provide another opportunity for the priest to be seen and known by the children.

One of the more increasingly popular ways for the priest to minister to the children and their families is through a special Family Mass on Sunday, perhaps once a month, which would include a special homily for the children. This is done in many parishes on Christmas Eve, but doing it at least monthly emphasizes the fact that they should be coming each weekend, not just on special occasions. These monthly celebrations bring the families together in a special and significant way, illustrate the parish's concern about the upbringing of their children in the Faith, and often provide an opportunity for some of the children to not only serve Mass but also be trained to be Lectors and ushers at that particular Mass.

If possible, there might even be a Children's Choir to lead the assembly in sung prayer. A gathering after the Mass with refreshments provides one more opportunity for families to get together in an informal setting, to meet the priest "outside the sanctuary," and to build the spirit of the parish among its younger members.

At a time when many people don't feel they "belong" to a parish—or to anything, for that matter—these practices can go a long way toward building a strong and active parish family.

CHAPTER 19

The Priest and
the Elderly

It is a well-substantiated fact that the number of senior citizens in our nation is increasing every day. The dedicated parish priest will acknowledge this fact and respond to their needs to the best of his ability. These needs can be on several levels. The most obvious would be those who are home-bound and therefore unable to participate in parish liturgies, activities and programs. So there must be developed a constant sense of outreach to them at whatever age they might be.

Very often, these are the people who literally built the parish church or, if not, were active participants in the life of the parish for a number of years up to the time when they could no longer be active. A monthly visit from the parish priest does so much to help those persons retain a vital interest in the life of the parish. He can bring them Holy Communion, hear their Confession, and see that they receive a copy of the weekly parish bulletin so as to be up-to-date in knowing what's going on in their parish. The parish priest can also train a group of Extraordinary Ministers of Holy Communion to bring the Blessed Sacrament to these people on a weekly basis, especially if the shut-in was a regular recipient of the Eucharist at Mass. If these Ministers can also be senior citizens, then the relationship between such contemporaries often enhances those visits and fills a need of both parties, the one who serves and the one being served.

Today it is a rare parish that does not have at least one home for the aged or an assisted living complex within its boundaries. The occupants are often former parishioners or non-parishioners now living within the parish boundaries. Contacting the Recreation Director about going to the facility to offer Mass at least once a month usually brings a very favorable response, thus opening the door to reaching out to another segment of the population that can be easily forgotten. This, too, can be enhanced by weekly visits by the parish group of Extraordinary Ministers of Holy Communion. Very often, the parish priest has only to ask for volunteers to do this, but it still is important for him to celebrate the Mass for the residents at least once a month. These are people who, as they grow older, think more and more about "their days dwindling down to a precious few." They need—and have the right to—the great reassurance and consolation that comes with at least a monthly participation in the Mass. I can personally assure the reader of the deep sense of gratitude these people express to the priest for his taking time out to provide this service. Since they are sometimes the sole surviving member of their family, his presence in their midst reassures them that they are not forgotten.

But what about those who are not shut-in? How can the priest serve them? When I first arrived at the parish that was to be my final pastorate, I inquired about what was being done for the senior citizens. I was told that the town had two excellent programs that we could not afford to match, so I put aside the idea of inaugurating a parish senior citizens program. Later on, a little research uncovered the fact that a number of those who attended the town-sponsored or AARP programs were able to do so because the town provided transportation for them. However, because those same people lived alone and were not provided town transportation on weekends, they could not come to Mass. Moreover, because concern about insurance liability in case of an accident made many parishioners hesitant to bring the home-bound to church, it became difficult to find individual persons who would transport others to church. Therefore, we arranged to bring them Holy Communion once a month at the centers where they met during the week and they were most grateful.

Several years later, a group of older people asked if they could start a program for parishioners that would feature religious activities including visits to some of the shrines within a one or two day's journey of the parish. I gave them the go-ahead and within a few months they had a membership of one hundred fifty and a waiting list! It was another instance of listening to and empowering the laity and one which brought many of them closer to the Church.

A word about that expression, "empowering the laity." Among the important documents that were produced at the Second Vatican Council is the *Decree on the Apostolate of Lay People.* This work should be studied by all priests and the laity so they can understand more clearly the essential role they are to play in the life of the Church. Suffice it here to quote from the Introduction: *"The need for this urgent and many-sided apostolate is shown by the manifest action of the Holy Spirit moving laymen today to a deeper and deeper awareness of their responsibility and urging them on everywhere to the service of Christ and the Church."* The document goes on to develop that need by reviewing, as we already have done, the implications of the Sacraments of

Baptism and Confirmation which the laity have received. No longer are they only to "pray, pay and obey"; rather, they are to play an essential role in the work of evangelization and the administration of their parish. Witness the absolutely essential role they fulfill in spreading the Faith in the parish Religious Education programs, the administration of the parish as members of the Parish Council, the Finance Committee and even as Parish Administrators where the absence of, or the overwhelming load placed on the pastor is a fact of life. The document goes on to point out the role of the priest as the source of the development of the spiritual life of the laity, so that they look upon the role as a real part of the apostolic mission of the Church and not just someone "doing a job." I can personally attest to the fact that when I retired from being a pastor of a very large parish, there were seventeen different programs or activities that were up and running successfully without any direct involvement of any of the priests. I received periodic reports on what was taking place but it was the laity who not only participated in them but also directed them. Without such lay involvement, many of the great works coming forth from today's parishes would simply never happen and the Church would be much less effective.

CHAPTER 20

The Priest and
the Poor

There are very few lines in Scripture as clear in its implications as the one from Matthew in which Jesus says, "As long as you did it for one of these, the least of my brothers and sisters, you did it for me." What is it we are supposed to do? Feed the hungry, give drink to the thirsty, clothe the naked, give shelter to the homeless, visit the imprisoned, and care for the sick. Indeed, it is on these actions more than any others that we will be judged as being worthy to enter eternal life in heaven.

One of the most outstanding results of the social teaching that emerged from the Second Vatican Council is the number of social justice projects now being undertaken by churches throughout our land. They take many forms: soup kitchens, overnight shelters, immigrant advocacy groups, outreach to the home-bound and/or to those whose lives are limited due to disabilities, Midnight Runs that bring food, clothing, blankets and toiletries to those who live on the streets of our big cities, Headstart and School Food programs, programs for those dealing with unexpected pregnancies, and similar activities. All are aimed at caring for those who are less fortunate than those who at least have life's necessities.

At one time or another in my half-century of priestly ministry, I have participated in all the above forms of service to the underprivileged, working alongside a whole army of very generous and dedicated religious and lay volunteers. Leading by example is clearly one of the best ways for a parish priest to inspire his people to acknowledge their blessings by sharing what they have received with those who have less. Such priestly ministry will also serve to strengthen the priest's own trust in God and an attitude of gratitude for all he has received. After all, from the day of our ordination, we have never had to be concerned about having a place to live, food on the table or clothing to wear.

However, there is another way in which the parish priest serves the poor and that is by his own personal involvement with them in a one-on-one situation. In a gathering of parish priests, if one brings up the topic of "those people who appear at the rectory door," there will follow one fascinating story after another. Some of them are heart-wrenching, some unjust, some frustrating, some hilarious, some ill-timed, but all of them real and many of them memorable.

There is quite an array of those who can be described as "con men" (and women). For example, there is the mother who needs milk and diapers for her children but the children are not with her because they are "staying with a friend"; the father who is out of work but "has a job lined up for next week and I'll pay you back then, Father"; the family that is traveling but ran into "unexpected repairs on the old car" (which is nowhere to be seen) and needs help to get to their destination which is always a good distance away; the person whose parent is dying in a distant hospital and they need the fare to get there; the emaciated person who quite obviously is a drug user but who just needs bus fare to get back to their family "to start fresh"; the person who has finally found an apartment and has the first month's rent but doesn't have the one or two month's security; the older person who has to have a prescription filled but whose plan (if they even have a plan) doesn't cover that particular medication and on and on and on. What is the parish priest to do?

There are those parishes that set funds aside for just such occasions and the priest, after a few encounters, learns what questions to ask in order to try to get to the truth, something not always accomplished no matter how astute the questioning. The parishioners usually contribute to such a fund or the pastor puts a set amount aside each week from the collection to deal with such persons in need. Some parishes, especially those that are suburban or rural, have an arrangement with a local diner or the bus company and a phone call to either or both will secure a meal and/or a ticket, with the parish reimbursing the merchant later on. Wonderfully, such merchants often regard this assistance as an act of charity and gratitude to God that they can provide the assistance, and so perform these acts of charity without seeking any reimbursement.

However, not all parishes can afford to do this, so very often the priest reaches into his own pocket and helps out. "But what if the person is lying, Father?" some parishioners will ask. "What do you do then?" The first answer is obvious. If you determine that they are lying you let them know and then either deny their request or give them what you think is really needed. If the story is accepted but in reality is a lie, then that is the person's problem, not the priest's. The grace of God usually sends a message to the priest, a message heard in the gospels: "As long as you did it for one of these my least brothers and sisters, you did it for me." Far better to err on the side of generosity—even if the story is not true—than to turn someone away whose need is real.

My very first assignment was to a town in upstate New York, then the hub of a resort area in the Catskill Mountains. It was overflowing with expensive and mid-range hotels, bungalow colonies and a steadily increasing number of motels. The traffic in the town doubled or even tripled during the summer vacation period which meant a large number of workers had to be added to the staffs of the hotels and motels. It was the practice of several of those resorts to go down to New York City on Thursday, pick up a truckload of unemployed men from the streets, bring them up to work around the clock for the weekend, usually as dishwashers, then give them a small amount of money for their labor and turn them out onto the highways to find their way back to the city. Some would go back to the city but many would hang around the outskirts of the town hoping to make it through the week and then go back to work the next weekend. Often they got drunk and then appeared on the rectory steps looking for food and bus fare to go back home.

To respond to their need, we had an arrangement with the bus company and the local diner cited above. Part of the routine, of course, was the self-initiated promise by the man that he would pay us back for our kindness; I think that happened twice. However, we never considered our assistance to be a loan; it was simply doing what we felt we should do.

One weekday afternoon, a young man, well-dressed and well-spoken, appeared at the rectory door. He told me that his mother was critically ill in Massachusetts General Hospital and that he had gone by bus from his home in Tennessee to see her.

He even showed me a letter from the hospital testifying to his mother's serious illness. He also stated that he had a brother in the Josephite Fathers religious order. His story was that, after visiting his mother for a few days, he began his journey back home to Tennessee to resume his job. He boarded a Greyhound Bus to New York and wanted to take a nap so he put his coat over the seat in front of him while he rested. When he arrived at the terminal in New York City, he picked up his coat only to find that someone had taken his wallet from the coat. He then went to a trucking firm to see if he could hitch a ride on a cross country truck. He did so, having been told that the truck was going West but it actually went Northwest which brought him ultimately to our rectory door. He needed thirty-five dollars to get some food and a bus ticket back home. (Remember—this was in 1957!)

After quizzing him about a few details in his story, especially about his brother the Josephite Father, I was convinced that he was telling the truth, wrote out a personal check for $35.00 and even called the local bank manager, a parishioner, authorizing him to cash the check. Uttering profuse thanks and promising to pray for me, the young man went happily on his way leaving me feeling quite good about being so generous to a man in trouble. After all, wasn't that what a priest was supposed to do? Wasn't that what Jesus would have done?

Two years later, I was on our annual priests' retreat at the seminary and, during one of the breaks, a group of a dozen or so of us priests started sharing stories about the people who come to the rectory door. It did not take long for us to realize that, if there were fifteen priests in that room, the young man with the brother who was a Josephite priest had hit at least ten of us! But there was a lesson to be learned from one of the older men in the group. He, too, had encountered the young man but thought that it was worth a phone call to the Josephite headquarters to find out if there really was such a priest. The answer was, "No, and we would very much appreciate your doing whatever you can to get this man out of circulation because he is doing our reputation no good!" So the older man wrote out a check for $35.00, sent the young man on his way, then called the local police who caught up with him just as he boarded a train to the next town. They searched him and found a handful of similar checks in his pocket. We priests all had a good laugh at that but we also learned a good lesson.

Did we all learn it? I can't speak for the others but I know I have been "taken" a number of times since then, occasionally for a lot more than $35.00, and have learned to deal with it as indicated above. If the person is lying, then it is his sin, not mine, and if he is telling the truth, then I have helped someone in real need. Case closed.

This part of a priest's ministry, if carried out with a truly generous heart, also reveals to him the fact that God will not be outdone in generosity. I can personally testify to the fact that whenever I dug down into my own pocket (or wallet) to assist someone in need, some way or other that money would be replaced, perhaps by way of an unexpected Thank You gift, a Mass stipend, an unexpected donation, or another kind of gratuity. Indeed, there are times when I "dug deep" to help and then found myself waiting to see how the money would be replaced... and it always was!

Then there are the stories of failure no matter how great an effort one makes to bring about a successful ending. Emily was a frail mid-thirties woman who arrived at the rectory at the suggestion of her neighbor. She was the mother of two children, sick, broke and in desperate need of help. We provided what we thought would be of immediate assistance and thereby unwittingly opened the door to a long-term relationship. Over the next few months we paid medical expenses (she had no plan and in New York it often takes a minimum of forty-five days to get on the Social Services' rolls), food, small amounts of cash and moral support. We even provided her with a small TV set, one that was left behind by a previous parochial vicar. This kind of support went on for several weeks until we got suspicious of the authenticity of her plight. So we made a surprise visit to her apartment, concluded that she was a drug addict and decided to cut off all support unless she entered a rehabilitation program. She adamantly denied her drug abuse and refused to enter a program.

A few days later, she was arrested at a local department store for stealing cigarettes. She asked the local police to call me, telling them that I would explain her situation and they did. When I asked why they were arresting her for stealing a pack of cigarettes, they explained that she had been caught with twelve cartons of cigarettes stashed in the lining of her coat. Realizing that she was falling deeper and deeper into the pit of drug addiction, I agreed with them that they should arrest her and, if the judge so decided, to put her in the county jail. Her two children were now in the custody of her mother so she was sentenced to six months.

After about three months, I received a call from the warden commending me for practicing the tough love of letting her be arrested. (One will find that "tough love" is often just as tough on the lover as on the loved one.) He said that Emily was clean, had gained weight, was receiving medical attention and seemed to have gotten on the right track. Naturally, I was pleased.

At the end of her term, she arrived back at the rectory looking for some assistance to get settled in a new one-room apartment and we provided it. However, it was only a short time later that she called me from a local hospital. She had fallen back into her old drug habit and was in serious condition. I visited her, prayed with her, gave her the Sacraments and told her I would keep in touch.

A few days later she died and it was my sad duty to celebrate her Mass of Christian Burial with her mother, her two children and a handful of friends in attendance. From a medical and emotional point of view, our efforts to assist her had gone for naught. However, my prayer is that, in return for our ongoing generosity to Emily, the Lord also provided us with the opportunity to prepare her for her death. I continue to serve people like her, consoled in the hope that the sacraments I celebrated with Emily opened for her a swift journey to her merciful Lord.

There are many other stories that I and most parish priests could tell about the people who come to us for help. They challenge us to respond as we think Jesus would and, letting our hearts rule our heads, we often misread their situation or their intentions. Nonetheless, as we noted above, we would rather err on the side of practicing charity in some form than in sending someone away who, in reality, was truly in need of help. But let me conclude this chapter with my favorite story of my fifty years of parish ministry, one with an ironically humorous ending.

Dan O'Brien was a stocky, bespectacled little man around seventy years old. He lived in our parish, or so he said, but I was never able to get an exact address from him. He would come to the rectory from time to time, seeking some advice about a problem or two, ask for a modest amount of financial help, then disappear until he needed more counseling and/or assistance. Somewhat strangely, he always asked for a very specific amount, such as $42.25 or $29.50! Because he never failed to have a story that was at least engaging, if not of any great significance, I would listen with amusement, give him what he asked for and then he would move on. Moreover, whenever he would get sick, he would check into a local hospital, local, that is, to wherever he happened to be at the time, giving them a false Medicare number. He would usually do this on a Friday afternoon, knowing that the hospital would not be able to check the number until Monday, by which time he would have "recovered" sufficiently to leave the hospital without paying anything! It's called "working the system."

After a year or so of these encounters, he admitted to me that he was homeless and asked if he could use our address to receive his Social Security check. We agreed and over the next few months we received his monthly check which he would promptly pick up, together with a fistful of bills from hospitals throughout the metropolitan area. Those bills were then deposited in the corner trash basket after he left the rectory. Each time he arrived he would ask for me and we would sit down and chat, he would ask for some "supplemental" financial help and then go off to parts unknown. Then one day I received a call from an undertaker in Brooklyn (not a part of the New York archdiocese). I was told that Dan O'Brien had been found dead in a local park and, in going through his papers, the police found a paper indicating that I was the next of kin! I thought to myself,

"God bless Dan. He got me consistently in life and now he has gotten me in death!" So we buried him with full ceremonies and, to this day, I smile every time I think of him. Just one more example that when the rectory doorbell rings, it can be a very brief encounter or one that will carry a relationship that will go on and on, perhaps even until "death do us part!"

CHAPTER 21

The Priest and Suffering

One of the most frequent requests a priest hears is, "Please say a prayer for me, Father," and the priest proceeds to add one more name or cause to his "prayer chain" of requests. That's a good thing because it serves as one more link in the chain of connections that a parish priest can have with his parishioners; it also strengthens the person's conviction that the priest does have a special relationship with the Lord. However, whenever the priest responds to that request with one of his own, "And will you please say a prayer for me?" he either gets a response such as "You don't need prayers, Father. You have a special connection with the Big Guy upstairs!" or, if that is not spoken, there is at least a somewhat surprised look that reflects that inner thought. It is at those times that I recall once again the statement from the Scriptures, "To whom much is given, much is expected." In light of that statement, no one has been given more than a faithful priest and he is frequently reminded of that in a whole host of ways. However, precisely because of that statement, each priest has an ongoing need of the prayers of his people to help him continue to give what is expected.

While God provides him with all the graces he needs to fulfill his vocation, those graces do not erase the priest's humanity or the fact that he carries about within him—as does every person—the effects of Original Sin. He is a frail human being who not only needs God's grace but also the prayerful support of his people because he, too, carries crosses, suffers illness, can be affected by loneliness, may have a genetic disposition to an addiction, or struggles with shyness or a sense of inadequacy toward an assignment he has been given. He may be caring for a parent or parents or a sibling who, for whatever reason, have become his responsibility. He may be having difficulty interacting with parish staff member or be wrestling with a major decision about the life of his parish and once made, it may not sit well with some or even a goodly number of his parishioners. The hope is that the decision has been made after open discussion with the members of his staff and that he will then explain it to the people who will be affected by it.

On a personal level, I think immediately of my father, a very devout and highly intelligent Catholic who was an outstanding father and husband, who died at age 67 after spending the last fifteen months of his life in a hospital, unable to move a muscle from his neck down during the final nine months of his life. I think of my mother who lived as a widow for twenty-one years, then died just five days after suffering a massive stroke. I think of the first of my brothers to die who passed in a matter of seconds just after getting into bed at night, whose death shook the family because of how suddenly it occurred and because he was the second youngest but the first to die. I think of my youngest brother who, two years later, died of a heart attack after battling alcoholism for almost twenty-five years but who, praise God, was sober the last four years of his life. I think of my oldest brother, the "Patriarch," who died just five months later after almost two years in a home following a series of strokes which rendered him unable to speak. All three died within three years, the last two within five months of each other. Did I celebrate their lives? Of course I did, but I grieved deeply at their deaths while leading their families and friends through the wakes and celebrating their Masses of Christian Burial and interments. Within that span I also buried my two closest lay friends, a husband and wife who died within fifteen months of each other, so it should be clear that priests are very human and are not spared suffering and human loss.

There will be other times when the priest is not feeling well, is dealing with pain or a feeling of weakness, or is concerned about a doctor's recent evaluation of his medical condition. A priest tends to be very private about his health issues because he takes seriously the expectation of his parishioners that he will "be there" for them whenever they need him, even though it might be at quite a difficult time for him.

Without going further, it should be obvious as we approach the end of this book that, while called to live a uniquely privileged and therefore demanding life where his conduct is always under close scrutiny, the parish priest should strive, with the constant help of God's grace, to meet that demand to the best of his ability. Nonetheless, as we have said, he remains a "wounded healer" who is more aware than any of his people of how unworthy he is of his calling. That's why, as we noted in a previous chapter, that he, too, goes to Confession in order to receive the forgiveness of God and begin again to try to be the consistently good representative of Jesus which his people have every right to expect.

It should be said again that his people should try to remember in their daily prayers that their parish priest is human and do whatever they can to support him and his efforts to serve them well, just as he remembers them and their struggles in his daily Mass. Though all priests are not provided with the gifts and talents required to be a good administrator or pastor, the present shortage of parish priests requires that, unless some physical or emotional shortcoming automatically removes him from consideration, just about every priest ordained in our time will be appointed a pastor—and this perhaps only a few short years after he has been ordained. All the more reason why he needs to know that he is being supported by the prayers of his parishioners.

Recall that one of my favorite passages from Scripture comes from Romans 8 and says: *"The Spirit Himself tells us that we are children of God, but if we are children then we are heirs of God, heirs with Christ, if only we suffer with Him so as to be glorified with Him."* This statement points out the reality of suffering in this life, a condition resulting from the Original Sin of our first parents and, indeed, as Paul describes it, a necessary condition for our glorification! It follows that their Sin brought into God's creation all the disorder we witness in all of creation and is the root cause of all the troubles and evils that beset us from time to time during our lives. While suffering can result from our own actions, we must be clear in understanding that no form of suffering happens as a punishment from God for our personal sins. God does not punish us in this life. (Even in the afterlife, it is our own rejection of God in this life that leads to eternal punishment in the next.) Rather, it is God's role as our loving Father to strengthen us in our suffering and enable us not only to get through it but also to turn it into meritorious suffering that brings the reward of a deeper identification with Jesus, our suffering Lord.

It is important to note that, in the above quoted passage from his Letter to the Romans, Paul goes on to say, *"I consider the sufferings of the present to be as nothing compared to the glory that is to be revealed in us."* In other words, just as Jesus conquered sin and death by His suffering and then rose from the dead, so do we share in His conquest over death and sin when we join our sufferings to His. It is through our acceptance of whatever suffering besets us, our struggling with it and our offering it to the Father, that we enter into a deeper union with our crucified and risen Lord.

Many times when John Cardinal O'Connor was the celebrant at the funeral of a priest who had suffered before he died, I heard him say, "Jesus did not save the world by His teaching or His miracles, as important as they were. No, He saved the world through His Passion, Death and Resurrection, that is, through His suffering, which tells us that this priest we are burying was never more a priest than when he joined his sufferings to Christ's and offered them to the Father in these last months of his life." Together with his daily offering of the sacrifice of the Mass, that priest's sufferings took on enormous, even immeasurable power when they were offered in union with those of Jesus. Nor does that suffering have to be terminal. So the next time you ask your parish priest for his prayers and he asks for yours, I trust that you now understand that he really needs them.

CHAPTER 22

The Priest and Evangelization

C learly, one of the principal roles of the parish priest is to spread the Faith. As we have seen, this can be done through interacting with the youth of the parish whether they are found in the parish school, the religious education program or the teenage youth program, by sponsoring or conducting meetings with the young adults, and in marriage preparation not only for the non-Catholic but also for the Catholic who often needs an up-date on their faith and a reminder about its fundamentals. However, in addition to all the things above which deal with those who are already in the fold, there is the role the priest plays in responding to the non-Catholic who is inquiring about our Church, its beliefs and practices.

As a young priest I noticed that most of these conversions sprang from an impending mixed marriage and the desire of the non-Catholic to share the future spouse's Faith. The usual format was for the priest and the person to meet at regular weekly intervals at which they would work with the *Baltimore Catechism* and such books as *Father Smith Instructs Jackson*. At the conclusion of the instructions, the non-Catholic would be received into the Church in a rather private ceremony, perhaps attended by the fiancée, the families, a godparent and a few close friends. It was orderly, quiet and usually quite effective.

Since the revision of the celebration of the Sacraments following the Second Vatican Council, the introduction of the Rite of Christian Initiation of Adults (RCIA) has replaced that one-on-one format and has broadened the process so as to include an RCIA Team including a priest or deacon, a group of well-trained parishioners, a thoroughly prepared team leader and perhaps the parish director of liturgy and music. Some wonderful programs for training this team have been developed in order to assure that the process is carried out in its fullest.

One of the outstanding components of the RCIA process is the active involvement of the parish. This occurs not only through the parishioners who are on the Team but also during the liturgical celebration of the various steps that lead to the "night of all nights," the great celebration of the Easter Vigil. Along the way, the Rite of Admission, the Rite of Election, the Scrutinies and the weekly Dismissal of the Catechumens and Candidates during Lent can all serve to make the rest of those who are present at the Mass in which they are celebrated not only aware of the RCIA process but when these are carried out with dignity and clarity, they also reawaken in the Assembly a greater understanding and appreciation of what a great gift they have received in their own Catholic Faith.

Clearly, one of the greatest joys the parish priest can have is to oversee the work of the RCIA Team, to celebrate the glorious Easter Vigil and, through the very rich ceremonies that are his privilege to carry out, to warmly welcome new members into his parish through the Sacraments of Initiation: Baptism, Confirmation and Eucharist. This is followed by the Easter season's process of Mystagogia, a post-baptismal period of instruction during which further teachings of the Church are explained. During this period the priest can continue to share in the excitement and joy experienced by all who participate. He can also deepen his relationship with these new members in order to assure them of being truly welcomed and to prevent the feeling of "graduating" from the process and then being left alone to grow—or not grow—as a member of the community.

When properly understood, the RCIA can be seen as the way in which the Church will now fulfill its primary purpose, to spread the Good News that is Jesus and to bring all people into the one flock of the Good Shepherd, the Catholic Church. It is not just a tool for the conversion of individuals but the way in which the Church will continue to reach out to the unchurched or those in other religious persuasions and it is to be done through *all* of its members, not just those on the Team. It is the role of every Catholic to reach out to those around them and do whatever can be done to bring those people into the unity for which Jesus prayed. The RCIA also provides to the faithful parishioner a time to reflect upon the gift of Faith that is theirs while witnessing the process of conversion being lived out in those actually taking part in the entire process. The pastor, the shepherd of the flock in his parish and the one specifically ordained to evangelize, will be the energizer necessary for bringing this about and by his prayers and leadership will set the tone that will produce the enthusiasm for the RCIA to succeed in his parish. There are, of course, exceptions to this process, namely those in which the potential convert is prepared individually and not in a group.

One of these provided me with a unique and memorable experience. It revolved around a brilliant world-class pianist about whom I first learned when I was a child growing up in New

York City. We lived just two blocks away from the Juilliard Music School which I and my older brother, Jerry, attended as children. (We were "practice pupils" for those students taking classes in piano pedagogy.) It was then that I first heard the name William Masselos or, as he was called because of his child prodigy status, "Billy" Masselos. He graduated from Juilliard, then went for a further degree to the School of Music at the Catholic University of America in Washington, D.C. which launched him on a brilliant concert career during which he performed with the finest orchestras in the U.S., Canada and Europe. Our paths crossed briefly at the national convention of the National Catholic Music Educators Association (NCMEA) in New York City in 1974 when he performed at a special concert with the New York Philharmonic Orchestra at Philharmonic Hall (later Avery Fisher Hall) at Lincoln Center. I was then the chairman of the New York Unit of NCMEA so I dealt with him directly. His was a remarkably dynamic performance of the Saint-Saens Piano Concerto, one that I will never forget for its sheer virtuosity. In ensuing years, I would read an occasional review of a recital he had given and the comments were always highly laudatory.

It was many years later that I received a call from Dr. Elaine Walter, a good friend who was at that time the Chairman of the Music Department at Catholic University, telling me that Mr. Masselos was now living in an apartment in New York City, was suffering seriously from muscular dystrophy and wanted very much to become a Catholic before he died. Since he was living not far from my residence, Dr. Walter asked if I would visit him and instruct him. I found him in an apartment on the upper West Side of Manhattan under the care of a gracious black lady who tended to his every need. He was seriously crippled as a result of his illness and had considerable difficulty speaking.

How contradictory was the setting in which I found him: here was this world-class pianist, unable to control his body, sitting in a living room graced by a full-sized Steinway grand piano. The irony of the situation was forceful and contained in itself a great life lesson.

While Bill found it difficult to express himself, he was extremely receptive to my visit and eager to do whatever was required to meet the fundamental conditions for his reception into the Church. Given the fact that he had been baptized into the Orthodox Church, the requirements were minimal and after a few sessions of reviewing with him the basic teachings of the Church of Rome, we set the date for his admission. It was celebrated at the Church of the Holy Name of Jesus in Manhattan and several of his closest friends were present, including Dr. Walter who had made the initial contact with me. Not long after, Bill Masselos passed away, a passing that marked the end of his suffering and the hoped for beginning of his life in heaven. How pleased and happy I was to have been privileged to prepare him for his admission to the Church and then to receive him into full union, especially since I had known of him since my childhood! Once again, a parish priest was made very much aware of the mysterious plan that God has for each of us and how grateful I am that this story included me precisely because I am a priest.

CHAPTER 23

The Priest as Administrator

Whenever I meet members of St. Patrick's Parish in Yorktown Heights, N.Y. where I served as pastor for twenty years before retiring, they inevitably ask, "Do you miss the parish?" to which I respond, "No." Surprised at my answer, they usually ask, somewhat in disbelief, "Really?" Then I go on to say, "I miss many of the people in the parish but not the parish." That's when they come to understand that my "No" refers to the administrative chores and duties which consume so much of a pastor's time, not to the people of the parish, many of whom are still very dear friends. Indeed, it was for the *people* that I labored enthusiastically and gratefully over those twenty years of my pastorate as well as for all the years of my priesthood.

The burden lies in the daily grind of being responsible for the maintenance, personnel and finances of the parish that I do not miss at all. These, as I view them, are not the stuff of which a pastor in today's Church should be the master or even the practitioner. While I considered myself a fairly successful administrator, it was primarily because of the excellent training

I received from several of the pastors with whom I had served, as well as the outstanding members of my staff who were so dedicated to keeping the parish functioning at its highest level of service. Truth to tell, although I gave it everything I had, I never truly enjoyed the administrative work for several reasons. First of all, on some occasions it took me away from the ministry to the people for which I was ordained. Secondly, without the help of wonderful secretaries, bookkeepers and maintenance men, I would not have been successful, so administrative duties could have been an occasion for disillusionment and even feelings of failure. Indeed, it was because the administrative duties became overwhelming in a parish "plant" that consisted of nine buildings spread over eleven acres, that halfway through my pastorate I hired a retired civil engineer to oversee the maintenance of the entire operation. I made clear to him that I would be available for consultation and would continue to provide input and suggestions, but the daily operation was no longer mine and I was free to deal with a steadily growing number of people and not things. When other pastors asked how I could afford his salary, I explained that in the first year of his supervision, he had saved me most of his salary by renegotiating contracts with the copy machine people, the computer people, the oil company and other vendors precisely because he was far more conversant with what those things should cost and what kind of contracts could be drawn than I had time to find out.

For example, in my last few years as pastor, we erected a Parish Family Education Center. I raised the money by conducting a campaign for which all the publicity was developed in-house, while he represented me at every meeting with the architect and builder. I was free to be a pastor, a shepherd of my people, while he did his job far better than I ever could have done it.

Suppose a parish cannot afford such a person on their staff. Then it could be possible for one such person to be shared by two or three parishes, with the maintenance staff carrying out the chores assigned by the Facilities Manager. Think of the hours of maintenance supervision that the pastor would be spared, which time he could devote to providing truly pastoral services. Of course, if such an arrangement is not possible, then the pastor will simply do the best he can, using the intelligence God gave him and calling into use the experience he has had. The real key is doing whatever it takes to see that the rectory staff members are the best people available and, just as important, that they get along well together.

While on this subject, given the increasing workload that is a heavy burden to so many pastors, I would strongly offer the suggestion that we need to rethink the whole job description of the pastor in today's Church. At the present time, we are probably ordaining twice as many permanent deacons as we are parish priests. In light of the array of professional experiences they have had in finance, personnel, construction, maintenance and other areas of the professional and business world, many of those deacons could assume at least some aspects of parish administration. They would be far more qualified than are the priests to function in these areas and thereby fulfill the original intent of the establishment of the diaconate, namely, to meet the material needs of the people while freeing up the priests to do what they were ordained to do: serve God's People in the whole host of ways we have indicated in the previous chapters.

This in no way would be a merely mundane use of the

deacon's gifts and talents since it would allow him to exercise a very important kind of stewardship on behalf of the parishioners. By seeing that the property and staff would be well used, they would be assuring the people of the parish that their investment of treasure, as well as time and talent, is properly and profitably used. This is just what many pastors have been trying to do, sometimes well, sometimes poorly for centuries, simply because they were appointed pastors. The deacon would then be using his expertise in a truly pastoral manner and accomplishing for the parish tasks that would often be beyond the capabilities of their pastor.

Another component of the administrative work of the parish is the Parish Council, an innovation in parish administration that came into existence following the Second Vatican Council. Of course, this can be a small group of the pastor's friends who simply "rubber stamp" his decisions, but that clearly is not what a Council should be. At the same time, the attitude that says "It's our parish, Father, and you should do whatever we tell you to do" is equally counter productive.

When I first arrived at my last parish, the Council consisted of representatives of the various organizations and ministries of the parish. The members were either appointed by the pastor or were chosen by the groups they represented. While this seemed to fulfill the purpose of a Parish Council, it soon became obvious that it was not very productive. Indeed, most of the meeting time was spent listening to reports of what was being done with little consideration as to how things could be improved and what additional things could be done. It was decided that we should conduct a study of the Council to try to determine how it could foster greater participation in the life of the parish on the part of many more parishioners.

In summary, the result was a change in our approach to the work of the Council. We came to see the parish not so much as an organization of several departments, ministries and activities—much as a business would see itself—but rather as a part of the Mystical Body of Christ. We saw it as an instrument for developing the spiritual life of the parish, as well as a tool for setting up a variety of committees that would address the overall life of the parish. From that time on there was a greater emphasis on the spiritual life of the parish and doing whatever could be done to involve more and more of the parishioners in the over all life of the parish. Some of the results were the selling and blessing of Advent wreaths, an annual Dinner Dance whose goal was not to raise money but to bring people together, a hospitality gathering after the Family Mass each Sunday, a series of talks on spirituality during Advent and Lent, and another on Challenges Within the Church Today, several pot luck suppers, the training of Special Ministers of Holy Communion, conducting Ministries Fairs to enroll more members, and similar programs and activities. Moreover, the number of Council members was set at fifteen and they are elected by the parish at large for a three-year term.

These changes have resulted in a much greater participation by more people in the life of the parish and lessening the load of work for the pastor, both good things.

CHAPTER 24

The Priest and
His Spare Time

In light of all that has been said, the reader may well wonder if the good priest has any time left for himself! Indeed, as the decrease in the number of priests continues, this is one of the primary concerns of the hierarchy, the diocesan health offices and the priests themselves. As one priest friend has put it, "While we're getting older and older and fewer and fewer, we are being asked to do more and more." I was once quoted in a national newspaper article dealing with this concern, "I go to bed tired and I get up tired," a situation subsequently confirmed by more than a few brother priests. It was only two years later on my 75th birthday that I opted out of my position as pastor due to burnout and so chose to retire. I just knew I couldn't do the required work effectively anymore or serve the needs of my huge parish according to my standards. Some asked, "Why not go to another parish as a senior priest?" and my answer was that, given my personality and relatively good health, I was quite sure I would find myself as busy as ever within a few months and I just was not up to it. It was, I felt, a good example that "the Holy Spirit tells you when it's time to go."

Dealing with a steadily increasing amount of work is a

181

problem that every dedicated priest has to deal with and there are several ways in which it is done. One is to establish the practice of taking a day off every week and sticking to it faithfully. That approach has worked to very good effect in the lives of many priests. They get out of the parish and visit family and friends or go to a movie, play a round of golf, visit a museum, go to a gym to work out or swim, or attend a concert and then end the day by having dinner with friends or brother priests. "Getting away" in this fashion pretty much assures his returning to the rectory refreshed and ready to resume his busy lifestyle.

Some priests are able to establish "a little place in the country" and go there on their day off to read, write, share a meal with other friends, and even have an overnight away from the busyness of the parish. I personally never arrived at either of those solutions, but made sure that I got out to dinner with friends at least twice a week and also took time to develop my hobby of performing Magic by reading, practicing and meeting with other hobbyists, something totally different from my otherwise priestly duties.

I also made sure that I took my four weeks vacation all at once so that it really was a time for re-creating my body and spirit. The last forty-three of those July vacations have been spent serving as a chaplain at Camp Marist in the White Mountains of New Hampshire where I had lots of time to pray, read, write, enjoy the Camp's marvelous facilities, and come home more than ready to begin another year of demanding parish life. So it really is a matter of "to each his own" for the physical, spiritual and mental health of each priest—and of his parishioners! Whatever the method, it is very important that there be some regular time of separation from his ministry so he can slow down, recharge his batteries and return invigorated to meet the challenges and properly deal with whatever awaits him.

CHAPTER 25

Humor in the Priesthood

Another entire book could be written on the many humorous or flat-out hilarious things that have been said either by, to or about priests. In reference to the former, some of the funniest remarks I have ever heard have been made by brother priests, often in the form of "inside jokes" but almost always arising from an ongoing sense of humor that actually can be viewed as a necessary component for anyone who hopes not only to be "successful" in the priesthood but also to experience the joy and personal fulfillment that should mark one's ministry of service. As for the latter, the funny things said to priests are legion and often punctuate stressful situations or reveal a lack of knowledge about Catholicism that can only be viewed as hilarious. Let me close with just one of these stories.

As a result of the generosity of the people of the parish, one year a few days before Christmas we were able to erect a life-sized Manger Scene on the knoll behind the church that faces a busy traffic intersection. So beautiful was this scene that for the first few days of its being in place, so many people came to view and photograph it that the town had to assign a police officer to keep the traffic moving.

However, one of the parishioners who was in the security business called me to ask what measures I had taken to prevent the theft of the figures. I was quite taken aback at the idea that anyone would do such a thing but he insisted. "All you need, Father, is for some inebriated character to decide to take the Baby Jesus home to his kids for Christmas and you'll have a problem." So to prevent such an occurrence, he said that he would come by the next day to run a thin but strong cable connecting the base of one figure to the next until they would all be on the one cable, thus making it impossible to remove any of them without taking them all. He would also install a security camera in the top of the manger. I reluctantly but gratefully acceded to his solution and then he added, "If you can clear it with the people in the house across the street, I'll have one of my men put his car in their driveway and sit in it through the night so he can keep an eye on the whole display." I sensed how serious he was so, rather than leave myself open to the possible theft that he feared, I again agreed to follow his plan.

That evening about eleven o'clock the rectory door bell rang and I went to answer it. There stood a young man in his blue uniform. "Good evening, sir," he began. (I knew when he called me "sir" that I was not dealing with a Catholic.) He went on, "I'm here to protect the display for the night." I thanked him and then said, "It's a very cold night. Can I give you some hot coffee or chocolate and a sandwich?" He thanked me indicating that he had sufficient food for the night but then went on to say, "But I think we have a problem already." Somewhat dismayed and a bit alarmed, I said, "Really? What could be the problem?" He stammered a bit, not knowing quite how to phrase his response, then blurted out, "The kid's not in the box!" Trying desperately not to burst out laughing, I smiled and said, "The kid doesn't go into the box until Christmas Eve."

Much to their delight, I shared the story with the parishioners the next Sunday and to this day, there are still several who recall that event each Christmas season and, when setting up the mangers both outside and inside the church, they never fail to ask, always quoting that thoughtfully naive young man, "Father, when do we put the kid into the box?"

CHAPTER 26

The Priest as the
Object of God's Love

I t is well said that God will not be outdone in generosity. If a person surrenders to His will, even if it is at considerable personal cost, God will more than compensate; indeed, He may well surprise that person with an experience he will never forget. It might follow a failure to achieve a personal goal, the loss of a job, the death of a loved one, the diagnosis of a serious ailment, the betrayal by a close friend or, in the case of a priest, an assignment he doesn't want to take, or some other emotionally devastating event. God's love is unconditional and eternal and He shows it to us daily in ways that we sometimes do not even recognize. In this final chapter, allow me to share two such events that were life changing to my own priestly ministry and revealed very clearly how God definitely has a plan for each of us, supports us in difficult times and often removes obstacles from our path, obstacles that we sometimes don't even realize are in our way. In such matters I would suggest He has a special concern for His priests.

Following my ten years of service as an assistant pastor in the parish of Immaculate Heart of Mary in Scarsdale, N.Y., I was assigned to my first role as a pastor at Our Lady of Victory in Mount Vernon, New York. (You may recall the story previously told about the call from the Cardinal just three days before Christmas.) My first visit to the parish was on December 28th, the Feast of the Holy Innocents. It was a bleak, rainy and cold day on which I approached a rectory that was in shambles. I would soon discover that the church was equally dilapidated and in serious need of redecorating. There was a large hole in the rectory porch, big enough for a child to fall through. About a third of the vinyl siding was missing from the side of the rectory, making the house quite unattractive and very cold in winter. The basement was cluttered with all sorts of useless articles and had a dirt floor on which huge water bugs scurried about. All the rooms, while clean, were in dire need of painting. The associate pastor then brought me into the church. I asked him to turn the lights on and he replied, "They're on!" and so they were. The Christmas decorations were dreary—except for the poinsettias—and as I gazed at the chipped plaster figures in the manger scene, I noticed that the ox had no ass! Having moved from a very well run parish where everything was in good repair and the rectory and church were always kept in fine condition, this "welcoming" was quite a jolt.

I soon discovered that the staff was quite capable and willing to help and the people were strong in their faith and unpretentious in their manner. Culturally, they were predominantly middle age and older Italian folk with a steadily increasing influx of Portuguese. The parishioners welcomed their new pastor and, content to let me run things in the style of a pre-Vatican II pastor, they took a pass on the idea of setting up a Parish Council. "You're the pastor," they said, "so you can make the decisions."

Within a year, and with money and a contractor supplied by the archdiocese, we were able to correct the defects in the rectory. When the clean-up was done, I recall one of the women saying, "Thank you for fixing up the rectory, Father. It's the home we provide for our priests and, frankly, we were embarrassed by it." Because a rectory always came with the parish, I had never viewed it in that way. Already they were teaching me.

In addition to making the necessary physical repairs to the rectory, there were other changes I attempted. I worked for eight weeks to teach the choir to sight read so as to be able to broaden their repertoire and they were fine when they were with me. However, once they returned to the choir loft and I to the altar, it was as though we had never even met. We purchased a new manger set but it was just a drop in the bucket when one viewed the need for a total renovation of the church.

Then there was the annual parish bazaar which a small devoted committee and I restructured to eliminate those volunteer workers who we discovered were "working" for themselves. I drove fifty miles north to find more attractive prizes and games than the carnival-type items they were used to. We tried to move the Bingo away from Friday and Saturday nights in order to make room for some weekend parish events, but the uproar from the Bingo regulars overruled that attempt—besides, we needed the money! We struggled mightily, to no avail, to increase the weekly collection offering above the $1,700 mark. There was even resistance to instituting some of the liturgical changes called for by the Vatican Council. So after a couple of years, I was getting tired of swimming against the tide of what I perceived to be negative influences and began to get angry, especially at God, for sending me to this backward place with its stupid people. I felt I deserved better!

In addition, during that time, I suffered a great personal loss when a very dear friend passed away from lung cancer. She and her family were my very closest friends, and her death in her early fifties was a very heavy blow to them and to me whom she often called, "my very best friend."

Meanwhile I had been invited to be part of a planning committee of members of the National Pastoral Musicians that was organizing a regional convention for church musicians and clergy in the Northeastern States. It was to be held in Providence, Rhode Island. I viewed the four three-day meetings in Woonsocket, RI as a welcomed escape from the parish.

The convention took place at the end of June but, as it turned out, I missed everything but the first night. The next morning at 3 AM, unable to sleep and experiencing severe stomach pains, I drove myself to the nearest hospital where my about-to-rupture appendix was removed at 7 AM. I returned home several days later only to develop peritonitis which brought me back to a hospital near the parish for more surgery. Soon after that, I made my annual trip to Camp Marist early in July but had to come home after only nine days due to physical weakness, and I then walked through the annual bazaar that I loathed.

The final blow came in mid-August when I was rushed to the hospital to have my gangrene-filled gall bladder removed. I had no previous history where my appendix and gallbladder were concerned—indeed, I have always been grateful to God for my very good health—and this final trip to the hospital put me over the edge. Now I was *really* angry with God! It was then that I learned that, while God doesn't cause illnesses, He certainly knows how to use them!

A few days after the gall bladder surgery, Msgr. Ed Connors, my former pastor and mentor, stopped into the hospital for a visit. He told me that he had just been appointed the Rector of St. Joseph's Seminary in Yonkers, New York, the archdiocesan seminary, and invited me to go there to recuperate. I thanked him but indicated that there were two or three families with whom I would prefer to stay. I thought to myself, "Why should I go back to the seminary? That's where this whole story started!" However, in God's plan, it turned out that none of those families could take me; two were going on vacation and the other was remodeling their home. So where did I end up? At St. Joseph's Seminary, of course, right where God wanted me to be! As Mother Teresa often stated, "If you want to make God laugh, tell Him *your* plans!"

The net result was that I made a much needed retreat and began to learn the meaning of "Let go, let God." I was there for almost eight weeks and during that time the Lord led me to realize that it wasn't "the stupid people" but *I* who was the block to His grace and the "stupid one" in that parish. Instead of leading them gently and trusting in their own deep spirituality, I was trying to force feed them to do things my way. With that newfound understanding and a recurring nudge from the Holy Spirit, I returned to the parish a changed man and from then on things really took off. Within a year, we launched a drive to renovate the church and, in a parish whose weekly collection averaged $1,700, we conducted a drive that raised $92,000 in eight weeks! People were withdrawing their savings and cashing in World War II Bonds! They loved their parish church that much. The renovation brought a whole new tone to the life of the parish and sent me and the people soaring, and when I was transferred from that parish to a much larger parish a couple of years later, a group of the parishioners thanked me "for giving us our parish church back." Little did they realize that, by their prayers, generosity, trust in and love for me, they had given me back my priesthood!

Having accomplished what we were able to do in rather surprising circumstances, I settled back, half-way through the fifth year of a six-year appointment, to enjoy our rejuvenated parish eighteen months before an evaluation would be done which would lead to either a six-year extension or a possible transfer to another parish. However, I was not to have either event happen because, once again, God had other plans for me. He is truly a God of surprises!

On Wednesday, May 8, 1985 I received a call from the Priest Personnel Director asking me to consider a transfer to what he referred to as "a biggee" in Yorktown Heights, a bit over a half hour north. I explained that my mother, who was now 89 years old, was suffering from, among other things, aplastic anemia which required her to enter the hospital about every eight weeks for blood transfusions. She was not doing well and I would prefer not to move any farther away from her. She was living on Fordham Road in the Bronx, about twenty minutes south of my parish in Mt. Vernon, and an assignment farther north to Yorktown would make it an hour trip to see her twice a week as I had been doing.

The caller went on to say that the change would not be for another four months and asked that I come down to the Chancery Office to review the profile of the parish and take a trip up to see it. He stated that the pastor there was a wonderful priest who had taught me English in my freshman year at the prep seminary and was suffering increasingly from diabetes. So, in response to his request, I said that I would come down on Friday.

The very next day, Thursday, the woman who was caring for my mother called to say that she couldn't understand what

Mom was saying. Knowing that this had happened once before, I surmised that she was overdue for a transfusion because no hospital bed had been available the previous week, so I went to her apartment and took her to St. Luke's Hospital in Manhattan. She was admitted. I stayed awhile, anointed her and returned to the parish. The next day I picked up the information about the parish in Yorktown Heights and drove north to take a look at the "biggee" and saw that it was a rather formidable situation.

On Saturday, I visited the hospital to find that Mom had suffered a stroke the previous night and was unconscious. On Sunday, May 12th, Mother's Day, I visited her again and remarkably, she had regained consciousness and was able to understand me but was now paralyzed on her left side and unable to speak. We spent three and a half hours together, talking, laughing, crying and saying the Rosary. To say the least, it was a grace-filled and very emotional experience. The next day I was unable to get to the hospital because of a number of parish commitments but called to find that her condition had not changed. Then on Tuesday morning at 2:10 AM I got a call from her doctor telling me, "Dermot, it's over." My response was, "Thanks be to God." Mom had always wondered, "When will Blessed Mother take me home?" She now had the answer.

The next three days were filled with all the arrangements for the wake, the Mass of Christian Burial and interment. My brothers and their families were summoned and many friends notified. Twenty-eight priests concelebrated the Mass and several accompanied my family to the burial. On the way, I could not help but reflect on how blessed Mom and I both were because we had been spared a long convalescence. She was well prepared to meet Our Lord and His Blessed Mother to whom she had a deep lifelong devotion. More than that, in just five days after that call from the Priest Personnel Office, the way was cleared for me to accept the assignment to St. Patrick's where I would spend the last twenty years of my parish ministry, a period of enormous work and growth and great fulfillment. Once again there came that message, "Let go, let God."

When the appointment finally became public, a friend of mine asked, "Aren't you concerned about moving from a parish of 475 families to one of 3,400?" The only answer I could give was, "When the Holy Spirit is breathing down your neck, you go where He tells you to go." In the next twenty years St. Patrick's would grow to 4,700 registered households.

Those are just two of the events in my life that taught me quite clearly how God first calls a man to priesthood and then guides him to wherever He wants him to go to do His will. It is not always where the man wants to go and sometimes he wonders just what God is up to, but he goes anyway. If the assignment is approached with an open heart and mind, it is always precisely the best place for that priest to serve God and His People at that time in his life. Simply put, because the parish priest is called by God Himself to be His eyes, voice, hands and heart, the priest is truly the object and more, the beneficiary of God's unconditional love in a very special way, as the Lord often accomplishes through him things that he never thought likely or even possible.

CHAPTER 27

Some Concluding Thoughts

Having shared all the above, I come to some concluding thoughts about your parish priest as a man of mystery. Originally, I divided his life into two levels of "mystery," that which pertains to the divine mysteries he is so privileged to celebrate and share, and then the "mystery" of what the rest of his life is all about. However, I hope that along the way you have discovered several other "mysteries," such as who is called to priesthood, how he is called, what influences that call, and how the Lord is always working with and through His priest to bring His message of salvation to all whom His priest encounters.

There is the further "mystery" of how the Lord works through the priest's sinful humanity, overcomes his weaknesses, puts him where He wants him to be, places people in his life whom he needs and who need him, strengthens him in times of challenge and suffering, protects him from himself and others who would turn him away from the proper carrying out of his ministry, inspires him at times of questioning or doubt and, in general, molds him into the priest He, the Great High Priest, wants him to be.

It should be further understood that the priest, still only human, may not always live up to God's expectations, to say nothing of those of the people. All of this places him in the same category as the rest of humanity because, truth to tell, all of us, priests, religious and laity are people who are on a lifelong journey, struggling each day to know God's will and to do it to the best of our ability in whatever circumstances we find ourselves.

Finally, it is my hope that the reader has had a consciousness raising experience that has led to a greater appreciation, perhaps at a deeper level than ever before, of how essential the parish priest is to the life of the Church and her people, and how important it is to face head-on the present critical shortage of priests in America. To recount the reasons for this shortage would serve little purpose here. Rather I hope that two things will result from this presentation.

The first is that *all* the People of God will understand the necessity of both praying for an increase of vocations to priesthood among our youth and then of inviting and encouraging the young men they know to consider whether God is calling them into His service. Those prayers and that invitation are *essential* to turning the tide and watching our seminaries reopen to prepare those who respond to God's call to embrace the work of the priesthood for the sake of the Church and the world. If the Catholic Church is to make the impact on our society that is so very much needed, then one of the principal ways will be through a growing and energetic corps of dedicated and happy priests.

The final hope behind this work is even more direct: that a number of young unmarried men will come to a clearer understanding of how very fulfilling and happy the life of a priest can be. In a society that measures "success" by how much one makes, owns or leaves to his heirs, there is a greater need for understanding how living the life of the parish priest can bring a sense of completeness and godly success that can be found nowhere else but in the priesthood. I pray daily for an increase of vocations to the priesthood so that the work of the Church may not only continue but flourish. It is my deepest hope that what I have presented here may encourage more young men to consider having the same glorious experience that God has granted to me and that the People of God will support them in every way possible, most especially with their prayers. What will he leave to posterity? Quite simply, a legacy of loving service to God and His Church and a long list of people who will always remember him and never stop thanking him for being in their lives when they really needed him. Could anyone ask for more?

ST PAULS

This book was produced by ST PAULS/Alba House, the Society of St. Paul, an international religious congregation of priests and brothers dedicated to serving the Church through the communications media.

For information regarding this and associated ministries of the Pauline Family of Congregations, write to the Vocation Director, Society of St. Paul, 2187 Victory Blvd., Staten Island, New York 10314-6603. Phone (718) 982-5709; or E-mail: vocation@stpauls.us or check our internet site, www.vocationoffice.org